MIRACLE CHILDREN
The Toybox Story

Miracle Children: The Toybox Story

The powerful story of changed lives on the streets of Guatemala

Duncan Dyason with Clive Price

Hodder & Stoughton
LONDON   SYDNEY   AUCKLAND

British Library Cataloguing in Publication Data
A record for this book is available from the British Library

ISBN 0 340 72184 7

Typeset by Avon Dataset Ltd, Bidford-on-Avon, Warks

Printed and bound in Great Britain by
Clays Ltd, St Ives plc

Hodder and Stoughton Ltd
A Division of Hodder Headline PLC
338 Euston Road
London NW1 3BH

Dedication

This book was written for the glory of God and in memory of all the street children I have known, played with, cuddled and loved, but who have been unjustly taken from this world.

Words can never express my thanks to my dedicated and wonderful wife, Jenni, who has stood by me since the first day we met, has never faltered, always served, loved unconditionally and has shown me the love of our Saviour.

'Now to him who is able to do immeasurably more than all we ask or imagine, according to his power that is at work within us, to him be glory in the church and in Christ Jesus throughout all generations, for ever and ever! Amen' (Ephesians 3:20–1).

Contents

Foreword

We stood, the four of us, in a sort of silence . . . with the noises of Guatemala City receding on to the back burner of our awareness. Behind us lay the city rubbish dump with its vast acres of rotting refuse, and covered with scurrying masses of adults and children: the outcasts of humanity, and all desperately seeking something – anything – recyclable to aid their attempts at personal survival.

In front of us was a block of graves, stark amid the heat and grime of the cemetery. The focus of our attention was a simple marker, just one among many, and dedicated to the memory of a child. It bore a plain inscription: 'Ruben Garcia', and the words, 'They called me a street child, because that is where I grew and lived, but nobody asked me why.' It was at that moment, as I looked at Duncan and saw the hurt and the deep compassion in his eyes, that I really began to understand the strength of feeling that had driven him and Jenni to devote so much energy and so many years to their work among the unwanted, the lonely, the injured, the rejected, the homeless, the dispossessed, the at-risk, the solvent-dependent – those who are the 'street kids' of this Central American country.

As we turned and walked away from that graveside, tears ran for a moment down my face . . . tears of sadness for a child's life cut short by police brutality and ignorance, but also tears of gratitude that at least one young family was prepared to face the pain of the streets. In doing so, they were enriching the lives of children who would otherwise continue in suffocating desperation, and ignorant of God's Son, Jesus, who died for their freedom.

I have known the Dyasons for a good number of years now, and am glad to count them as friends. And I'd like you, by reading this book, to get to know them a bit as well. But – and it's a big but – you need to know that there is a risk to reading this remarkable story. It may well change your life! It carries a complacency warning, telling of the ways in which God deals with and uses the ordinary people of this world. People just like Duncan, Jen and Katelyn. It reminds us of the truth that, at times, holy fools rush in, only to find that they are treading on the toes of their guardian angels. It nudges us into remembering that provisions are made, time and again, for those who are prepared to live their lives in a place where they are forced to trust God. It encourages us to encounter the God of the Bible, who is the God of the miraculous. It prompts us to remember that Jesus constantly lived his life among those who lived on the fringes of 'acceptable' society: the deprived and the disadvantaged. And it reminds us that he continues to live through his people in the desperate places – the fringes of our so-called 'respectable' society. It challenges us to get involved, not necessarily on the streets of Guatemala, but at every level of society in this deeply wounded and hurting world. Someone once said, 'Don't tell us that God loves us until you're prepared to love us too!' Duncan, Jen and young Katelyn have earned the right to tell the street kids of Guatemala that God loves them, because they have been prepared to love them as well.

A few days on from the cemetery experience, I stood,

this time in anything but silence, in the dining hall of Emmanuel, the boys' home high in the hills above the smog of the city, and I cried again, this time for sheer joy, as I watched Duncan in the midst of a handful of well-clothed and well-fed boys, now in the care of lovely Guatemalan 'parents'. The boys were bright-eyed with excitement, laughing, playing, and clambering all over this visionary young man, who had shown them at no little personal cost that Jesus is indeed alive today in Guatemala City!

Now you can read the story, although it is by no means at an end; like all the best tales, it is 'To be continued . . .'

Stuart Pascall

Introduction

I sat down next to him and told him my name. He seemed unconcerned who I was and what I wanted. All he was interested in was another sniff from his bag of glue. A small group of street children began playing a game of football in the alley that was littered with rubbish and human excrement.

The ball landed on my lap. I picked it up and tossed it to the children. It was soft and made of plastic and had obviously landed in numerous piles of excrement which had disguised its real colour. The boy I was seeking to communicate with was thin, aged about twelve, with black hair and glazed eyes. Eventually he told me his name. It was Ruben.

Only later did I find out that Ruben was a runaway. He had grown up in a home where his father would often beat him. One day his father hit him so hard he ran away from home and never went back. However, he did maintain contact with his mother, whom he often saw in the market-place.

The following week I saw Ruben again and, pulling up an old cardboard box from the rubbish pile, sat down next to him. This time he was more eager to talk and had obviously not had too many bags of glue that day. His face was brighter and he was concentrating on what I was saying.

'Ruben,' I said, 'I know that your life has been hard in the past. But it doesn't have to be that way in the future. You can make something of your life if you just put some effort into it.' I could see he was listening to what I was saying, but while wanting to believe it was possible he couldn't leave what he had come to know as his home, his family, his life.

'We all die, you know,' he replied. I looked at his face. He was looking at his feet, which were black and covered in dirt, oil and sores. He began picking at his toes as I looked up to see the other children beginning another game of street-rules football.

'But Ruben,' I said, 'you don't have to live like this, you don't have to die like the rest, you're smart and can choose a different path. Besides, God will help you if you ask him.'

'Come on, Ruben,' came a shout from the alley where the children were playing. Ruben stood up and wandered over to where the action was. I saw Ruben only a few times after that evening. The last time I saw him, he was dead in a crude wooden box.

Ruben and two friends – Daniel, who was ten, and Manuel, who was twelve – had found a place to rest for the night. Just two streets away from where I had been talking with Ruben, the boys found a shop doorway and began to huddle together to keep warm and to sleep.

No sooner had they fallen asleep than they were rudely awakened by a lady who was well known in the area for being somewhat mentally instable, and who began to shout at them. The boys sat up and listened to her screams. She was obviously accusing them of stealing from her that day and was now seeking revenge.

The time was nearly midnight, but even though it was late there were still many people coming and going from seedy nightclubs and 'hotels' in the vicinity. Within minutes the lady had quite a crowd of people around her as she shouted at the boys who, in return, were also shouting at her.

The small crowd and not so small commotion caught the attention of two private police officers who were patrolling the area. Approaching a lady in the crowd, they asked what was going on. She replied that these street children – referring to them as 'street scum' – had attacked the lady who was screaming and had robbed her.

The policemen pushed their way to the boys – who looked in horror as the policemen pulled out their guns and fired at point-blank range. Ruben and Daniel slumped to the ground, dead. Little Manuel saw his two friends die and was overtaken by shock and fear which led him to run as fast as he could. He had made it to the middle of the street when two shots rang out. Manuel fell to the ground; he had been shot in the back twice but was still alive.

Within minutes, police cars arrived and the two private police officers, who were only in their teens, were arrested. Manuel was taken to the city hospital where he received emergency treatment and was diagnosed as not in a life-threatening condition.

I was made aware of the incident the following morning. The story had actually made front-page headlines but caused little concern or stir. I rushed to the city morgue where I was informed of the whereabouts of Ruben and Daniel. I then phoned two of our staff, Herbert and Mauricio, who met me at the funeral director's.

Another charity that helped street children had collected the boys' bodies and transported them here overnight. A small group of street children from Ruben and Daniel's gang were present and had kept vigil over their bodies all night.

I walked into the funeral parlour, which was nothing more than a bare room with coffins, barrels of liquids and two tables on which two cheap wooden coffins were placed. Many children came to greet me and tell me in detail what had happened only hours previously. In the corner of the room sat an old lady, doubled over in grief and crying quietly to herself. The children informed me that she was Ruben's mother.

They then walked me to the place where the boys were laid and showed me their lifeless bodies. In Guatemala, most coffins have a glass window so that you can see the body. I thought I would have preferred not to see the bodies, but was told to look by the assembled children as these were their friends, their comrades, their family.

I felt nothing but emptiness, and sought to comfort those children who were still crying and beating the lids of the coffins in anger and disbelief. It was obvious that Ruben and Daniel had died violently and their bodies were testimony to that fact. Very little had been done, if anything, to clean them up for burial.

I walked out into the street after a while to catch some air. The atmosphere inside was quite oppressive. Herbert and Mauricio were walking up the road with a couple of our volunteers. We greeted each other and then I suggested they allow the children to show them the boys' bodies.

'This is something I don't expect you will ever forget,' I told them as they walked in. It was a solemn moment coming face to face with the reality of street life, and I set my heart from that moment on to do all I could to prevent this ever happening again.

An hour later we were invited by the other charity and Ruben's mother to join them in the funeral procession to the cemetery, which was about one mile away. The coffins were placed in the back of a minibus and we walked behind it, carrying some of the flowers that had been bought and placed on their coffins.

It took about twenty minutes to walk the short distance to the cemetery. Once through the entrance barrier, the coffins were taken from the minibus and placed on the shoulders of some of the children, the workers and us. It was a privilege to be asked to help carry the boys to their final resting-place. As we came to the spot where they were to be buried, everyone started crying loudly. Daniel was taken to an upper level and Ruben to a lower level. Ruben's mother walked next to his coffin followed by the children, staff and volunteers.

I watched as Daniel's coffin was placed in its tomb in the wall. I was the only one present when he was buried. Then I turned away and walked down to the spot where Ruben was being buried. By that time Ruben's mother was in hysterics.

'No, Ruben, no!' she cried.

Within minutes it was all over. Both boys had been bricked in the tombs and flowers laid at the entrance. Just opposite the rows of tombs was a steep drop down to the place where the millions of tons of rotting rubbish from the city dump were being pushed. The large black vultures that soared above gave the place a sinister feel. It all seemed unfair, unjust, and I asked God why he had allowed this to happen. It was a mess and there was no other way of seeing it.

Guatemala is known best as the land of eternal spring, a very colourful country, rich in traditions, which has welcomed the modern world but not allowed it to destroy its roots and cultural heritage. The rising volcanic landscape is home to nearly eleven million people, half of whom are children and teenagers. But its outstanding natural beauty is often hidden in this country where violence has become commonplace.

My very first visit to Guatemala had been a dramatic eye-opener. The headline of that morning's papers read: 'POLICE ROB BANK!' Seventy per cent of all Guatemalans live in households with incomes of less than twice the cost of their basic foods. In the past 150 years, successive dictatorships and military regimes have suppressed the population and failed to distribute the wealth of the nation. It is estimated that up to 80 per cent of land in Guatemala is owned by no more than 2 per cent of the people.

There are abundant crops of coffee, cotton, maize, beans, sugar cane, bananas, pineapples, wheat and corn, which provide 60 per cent of the country's exports. Guatemala also has natural energy resources in hydro-electric power and oil reserves, yet still most indigenous people work for starvation wages, and 82 per cent of the population have no access to clean water and sanitation.

UNICEF estimate there to be in excess of 1,500 children living on the streets, mainly in the capital, Guatemala City. Most of the street child population is aged between five and eighteen, and are both victims and products of an unjust and exploitative system. Thousands of children were orphaned during the 1980s; others have been abandoned by parents too poor to feed them.

Some children are attracted to the streets by the apparent freedom and excitement that the city offers. These children are no different to those on the streets of London or any other major city of the world. Others have abandoned their homes because they have been physically or sexually abused by their families.

When the hunger and cold nights become unbearable, the children inevitably resort to theft or prostitution. Their average life expectancy is just four years. The children fear all adults, and regaining their trust is a major and rewarding achievement.

The security forces are the largest employers in the city. Two or three heavily armed police languish on street corners. Every bank is guarded by private police or the army, who carry automatic weapons. Corruption is a way of life. Armed guards stare out of doorways of many shops, including a children's clothes store and even a wool shop!

Seldom are police prosecuted successfully. Consequently there is no attempt to discourage those wishing to take the law into their own hands. The security forces have assisted victims of theft to administer beatings to guilty street children. Other children have been tortured to obtain 'confessions'. Supporters of trade unions have 'disappeared' and those who speak out have either received threats or been removed from this world. Guatemala has suffered under this legacy of institutional violence for the past thirty-four years.

Like cold and hungry animals, the street children hunt in packs. In order to survive in an adult world, the children are fiercely loyal to each other, but this loyalty can turn sour if the mood dictates and they fight bitterly over the most basic commodities. The children sleep huddled up together on the streets, sometimes during the day and sometimes at night.

They share their small quantities of solvents with each other, which gives them the courage to steal or to gang together to pick the pockets of the unsuspecting drunk. The price of getting caught is very high. On the streets there is really no discipline except within the group: there is no school to attend, no rules to obey, no routine to follow. The excitement is a 'free' life to do as you please and enjoy the camaraderie of the gang. The reality of their sordid existence is anaesthetised by inhaling glue or, more popularly, industrial and medical solvents.

Children asleep on the capital's streets are an embarrassment to the government. Tourists are deterred from shopping where dirty scruffy kids litter the pavement. The children themselves can be wild and threatening and take on a character which belies their young years.

Guatemalans can, and some do, marry at age fourteen. Consequently the police see a fourteen-year-old as an adult, not a child. The police have an expedient and ready solution to street child crime, knowing that no one cares anyway as they are 'only' street children. If you possess very little and some of your most treasured belongings are stolen by an irresponsible adult who is either an alcoholic or a solvent abuser, sympathy, love and compassion are not natural emotions for you. The children seem little concerned that one day they will have to face reality.

1

The First Miracle Child

'There's your things,' she screamed, 'what's left of them. It's up to you now. Find somewhere else to live.' I couldn't believe it. Scattered across the garden and the street were my clothes, my records – all my precious possessions. A friend had given me a lift home after work. As I got out of the car, my mum had shouted her proclamation from a window. And with that, she told me never to return. So that was it. I was homeless.

It had been a torturous route that had led to that point in October 1978. I remember always having been hungry as a child. Often I'd have to break into my own house to get food. When my parents went out they would always lock me and my sisters out of the house. So we made camps in the garden to live in until they came home again. We found a great way of getting into the house through the toilet window. We'd steal things that we thought wouldn't be missed, like cereals and cooking ingredients. But my parents would always find out. So then we'd have to go without food for ages – or receive a thrashing.

We had a little house that came with my dad's job. He was a gardener for a wealthy family and spent little time at home. My mum was responsible for discipline in the home. She seemed to take pleasure in using a horsewhip on us, standing us in corners for hours on end – at times with no clothes on. Making us go without food was always her favourite punishment. My two elder sisters carried the can most of the time. But when they left home, it was down to me.

It wasn't long before the education system had written me off, too. Between the ages of thirteen and fifteen I attended Woodroffe School. Set on a hill in Lyme Regis, it was a mixed secondary school with a good reputation. But I never enjoyed it.

I would often skip lessons and hide around school. Or I would walk down to the beach and wait until the end of the day, then hop aboard the school bus home. A couple of boys, Peter and Simon, befriended me and would often include me in their games. They'd even help me out if I struggled in the classroom.

Then there was John Hollis. For some reason, this English teacher believed in me. He was always kind. He made me think about life – and especially about things which gave me hope. But I found the rest of the time boring and irrelevant. Furthermore, I was disappointed to find that not all teachers were like Mr Hollis.

'And where are you going?' a teacher challenged me as I arrived at school one day.

'Into the classroom,' came my snide response.

That teacher decided he had other plans for this brat. He marched me to the boiler room where I was told to put on a pair of overalls. Once I'd done that, I was ordered to go around the school and collect litter.

That was to be my solemn task each day, as the staff had decided I was too disruptive. It suited me fine. I hated school anyway. And so I became public enemy number one. When anything went missing, teachers would often confront me and accuse me of taking it.

'If ever there was a conspiracy,' I thought, 'this is it.'

I fought the system. But at other times I'd just put my

head down and get on with it. School did nothing to help me feel that life was worth my best shot. Instead it reinforced in me the feeling that I was on my own. No one really understood what was going on in my life. So what was the point in telling them?

I became a danger to most living things. My main weekly household chore was to take our washing to the launderette with my little sister, Michelle. That was our Sunday morning ritual. It was the most boring job, as I watched the washing going round in the machines.

One Sunday, my little sister and I had just filled the washing machines full of our weekly washing. We were sitting down watching it go round – yet again. Then I noticed Michelle playing by the line of tumble dryers. The more I looked at her and the tumble dryers, the more I wondered whether she would fit inside one! Moving over to the dryers, I opened one and looked inside.

'Michelle,' I said, 'I just want to try something out. I want you to climb inside this dryer and see if you'll fit!' She looked at me as if I'd just arrived from another planet.

'I'm not climbing in there. You'll shut the door,' she replied, with a measure of wisdom.

'Trust me,' I said, 'I'm your brother.'

Somehow I managed to convince her that the dryer was a reasonable risk. She climbed in. I started to rock the drum around from side to side – which she really enjoyed! I couldn't quite get it high enough to send her right over, which I thought she would enjoy even more. So I closed the door, put my money in the slot and turned the knob.

Michelle started spinning. And for some reason, she appeared to be somewhat distressed. In fact, she looked out at me with real horror. So after a while I let her out.

That night I ached all over when my parents found out what I'd done. But at least I wasn't sent to the launderette again.

As I grew up I began to see a great disparity between the way we lived and the way everyone else lived. I began to see that if you stole things from people you could get things you wanted. So at age nine I started taking things from school, like pens and other stationery items. One of my sisters was already stealing a lot from school and would sometimes bring me things that she had taken. I noticed that it was easy. At least, it was easy if you didn't get caught.

When I was twelve I began to steal things from other people's houses – usually items left lying around in the garden, like bikes. Then I had an idea. It was to lead to my first brush with the law.

My mother used to collect money for the Royal Society for the Protection of Birds. Under the bed somewhere she kept a collecting-box shaped like a small, plastic puffin. I found it and took the box to school one day. On my way home, I knocked on people's doors and asked them for a 'donation'.

It seemed a safe routine. Every day I would visit a different road and collect more money. The takings, of course, were not spent on bird food and wildfowl sanctuaries, but on sweets and toys. I would hide the box in a hedge on my way home.

But a swift end soon came to my birdman deception. One afternoon I was standing outside someone's door waiting for an answer.

'Hey! What are you doing?' asked a policeman on a bike.

'Collecting for the RSPB,' I replied, with as much sincerity as I could muster (which wasn't much).

'Okay, then, let's have your name,' he said, 'and who gave you permission to do this?'

Silence. I had no script for that. So I said nothing. The constable asked me to go with him to the police station. There, he asked me my name and address. And still I remained silent. I kept that up for a good couple of hours until I gave in and told him who I was and where I lived.

A police car took me home shortly afterwards. When the car stopped I ran away. The policeman who had first apprehended me gave chase, but he was no match for my young legs. I soon made quite a distance between the two of us.

After a couple of hours' hiding, I slowly made my way back to the house. The police car was still outside. Clearly, evasive action was needed. I climbed over the back fence, up the drainpipe and into my bedroom through the window. So far so good. Unfortunately for me, I landed on the floor with a thud!

That brought both the policeman and my mum upstairs and into my room. My mum started screaming at me. And the policeman was obviously not happy. His boots were caked in mud from our previous chase across the fields.

The punishment didn't stop. My headmaster found out what had happened, too. He summoned me to his office and asked me to bend over. I got three whacks of the cane across my rear end. To say it stung was an understatement.

Over the following year, I went back for repeat courses of similar treatment – particularly after other students' property was found in my bag or something else went missing. It was clear I was being watched too closely at school. So I began to break into people's homes. I stole money, clothes and anything else I thought looked valuable.

Not far from home, I found a house where a downstairs window had been left open. I knocked at the door. No answer. So I climbed in. I went upstairs and into one of the bedrooms. Then I heard the front door open. The occupants had returned!

I saw them unload some shopping from their car while their two children began to run around the house. I don't know how I did it, but I just walked down the stairs and straight out of the front door. No one saw me as I wandered past the car, along the drive and out into the road.

Yet still it seemed as if someone was watching me. I felt quite spooked by this. Afraid, I decided to stop breaking into houses. However, that arrangement only lasted about two weeks. Then I decided to break into our next-door neighbour's house. That was my undoing. I was caught by the police, and criminal proceedings were brought against me.

I had a hunger for material things. And I enjoyed taking something away from those who had plenty. Even the police were losing all hope for me. They didn't think this lad would do anything else – apart from excelling at a life of crime.

Then one man stepped into the confusion of my world. He spoke up for me in court, as I stood in front of a judge who was threatening me with eighteen months' youth custody. I can't even remember this other man's name. What I do remember is that he was a social worker. And this caring, middle-aged man even seemed to know what I was thinking and feeling inside.

We met just after I had been arrested for breaking into my neighbour's house. Several other incidents were also taken into consideration. The court asked social services to produce a home study on me. So this man turned up at my home one day after school. We didn't start on the best of terms, as initially I thought he was the police.

But little by little he began to ask me about what I wanted to do with my life, what I liked and disliked, what school was like, what home was like, and so on. He came back after a week and we talked some more, which helped him produce a report for the court. Even after I was let off with a serious caution, he came back to visit me and see how I was. He was among the first people to show an interest. So I confided in him.

By that time, Mum and Dad had divorced. My father had left home when I was fifteen. As his sight was deteriorating rapidly, he went to a rehabilitation centre for the blind. He'd tried to visit my sister and me some time afterwards but my mother called the police when she saw him outside the house and had him arrested. My little sister was locked inside the house crying and I arrived home from work to hear that the police had been and Dad had been arrested. He returned to the rehabilitation centre confused and wondering if he would ever see us again.

Before long, I was back in court for burglary.

'This time, you won't get away with it,' my kind social worker warned me. 'If I were you, I'd be getting ready to spend six months in a youth custody centre.'

I began to pack my things. I wondered what life would be like inside such a place. But it was not to be. This man spoke up for me yet again, and had hatched a plan which the magistrate accepted! After some negotiations, my social worker informed me of the deal.

'You can work on a farm for one year,' he said, 'or spend six to eighteen months in youth custody.' I chose a year on the farm. I was actually looking forward to it. It meant leaving home for the first time. I was just fifteen at the time.

It turned out to be a painful year. Most days I would have to get up at 5.00 a.m. Then I would help get the cows in for milking. Then I would have to feed and clean out the pigs. Then I could have my breakfast. What I most enjoyed, however, was driving the tractors. In fact, I became fairly proficient at manoeuvring tractor and trailer in and out of difficult corners.

The family showed no interest in me. They were just pleased to have a free worker for a year. What's more, they really made sure that I was used to the full. During my whole year I had only a couple of days off. I would spend my free moments cycling round the cliffs and looking out to sea, just enjoying being on my own. But I always had that feeling that someone was watching me.

One day I'd cycled about two hours from the house when something went seriously wrong with my bike. I remember wondering how I was going to get back to the farm. I picked up the bike and began to walk. I came across a garage, and asked the mechanic if he could help.

Twenty minutes later he showed me the bike. He said it had needed a couple of new parts, but it was all now in good working order. However, I had no money on me. The folk who ran the farm never paid me anything during the whole year. The mechanic asked me to go into the office and see the boss, who had the bill.

The mechanic looked on as I gulped and walked towards the office. The boss came out from behind the counter and asked what I wanted. I explained that the mechanic had fixed my bike and that I wanted to find out how much it was going to cost. He left to talk to the mechanic and as he came back into the office, he quoted a sum of money. And I froze. Then his hand went on the counter and pulled a sum of money from near my hand. It was exactly the amount he'd asked for!

I stood there motionless. He rang the amount through his till. Then he wished me well. I walked out of his office, dazed and confused. 'What's going on?' I asked myself. I had that feeling again. Someone was watching me. But who?

I returned home. And I found that my mother was planning on making a move to start another 'new life'. She had the idea of a council house swap, to move from our home in Dorset to Lancashire. So we moved up to Blackpool to start afresh. There was just me, my little sister and my mum.

The council estate that we moved to seemed very quiet when we first arrived. That is, except for a notorious family who greeted us by shooting at our windows with air guns! The houses were all the same. Brick-built, three-bedroom homes displayed bare front gardens and backyards that had been relegated to dumping grounds. Most people's gardens had little or no boundaries. It seemed that our lives were mostly open to everyone's view. Old cars littered the streets, many in a state of disrepair. The streets were never at peace, especially at night.

Our home wasn't at peace, either. I had a few memories of good family times. But mainly I just wanted to die. My mum would drink and smoke. She'd try to embarrass me by inviting different men around all the time. When I was at home I would spend my time in my bedroom, trying to create another world where I would dream of being safe. When the shouting got too much I would wander the streets just passing time, or looking for opportunities to steal.

It was obvious I wasn't from the north, so the other young people hanging around the shops would ignore me. My motorbike was a way of escape. I would spend hours cleaning it and fixing it up. Then I'd ride it around the

17

housing estate without the exhaust attached in a bid to make as much noise as possible.

We'd spent all our lives moving from one house to another in search of work. We were also in search of a new start – or it seemed like it at the time. I knew that living with my mother again wasn't going to be easy. She found it hard coping with my moods, drinking and criminal activities.

Crime was now part of me. I was actually more afraid of relationships. That's because I thought they came at a higher cost. I'd locked all my feelings inside. And I was very good at not showing what I really felt. I knew there was no point in starting a relationship as I knew that it would hurt me if I ever did. The only relationship I had seen was my mum and dad's – and the time my next-eldest sister had a boyfriend. They would just sit on the sofa kissing for what seemed like hours on end. I didn't see any point in it at the time!

Relationships were bad news – particularly the relationship with my mother. I found it hard coping with my mum, who always wanted something else for me. She thought I was going nowhere as I didn't keep a job for long and didn't mix with the right company. She was also distressed to learn that I didn't have a girlfriend. She told me repeatedly that she reckoned I was gay.

I arrived home one day with a friend of mine to be greeted by a 'surprise' from Mum.

'It's waiting for you upstairs in your bedroom,' she said.

As I peered around the door, sitting on my bed was a young woman of about eighteen. She was a neighbour my mum had got to know. And she'd told my mum that she fancied me. So my mum tried to get us together.

'She'll teach you a thing or two,' said Mum. Looking back, as I did some time later, I thought about what would have happened if I had taken up the offer. But I was glad I didn't. Something inside told me it was wrong. However, my friend was next in line. He decided the opportunity was too good to miss. That encouraged my mum. And her reaction sickened me.

Obviously she had just about taken enough. I was nineteen when I was greeted by the sight of all my worldly goods scattered outside the house. My mum had thrown me out. And her cries echoed through my mind as I sat in the seat of my friend's car.

'So where to now?' he asked.

'I don't know,' I muttered. 'I have nowhere to go.' I was being honest. I felt desperate.

My friend drove me into the town centre. I started looking in all the newsagents' windows for adverts of bedsits. After a few phone calls I was invited to view a house-share. The place was small, dark and seemed to be home to about twenty people. The room was small, but cheap. I could move in right away. So I did.

The tenant in the room opposite was Peter, a twenty-year-old man who was openly gay. I made it very clear that I was straight. Then he became a friend. Each night he would go out to a gay club just around the corner, some nights he never returned. Early one morning I heard shouting outside my door. When I opened it I saw a group of police officers raiding his room, taking out books, magazines and videos. They asked me about Peter and said he'd been arrested for gross indecency. I never saw him again.

After a few months I was invited by Wendy, one of the girls in the house, to join her and her boyfriend in renting a small flat together. She'd left home as a teenager, and had experienced similar problems to mine with her own parents. She was a real laugh and would enjoy life to the full, always ready to help anyone in need. Because of her generous nature she would often be taken for a ride by everyone, especially boyfriends.

I thought this new move would further help in giving me a new start. My room was the attic. It consisted of two small rooms and I could share the bathroom and kitchen. It seemed great.

One day Wendy met a guy I worked with – Ian, who was from Scotland. They made plans to live together. At last she was happy and they seemed good for each other. The three of us got on well. Just three months before I left Blackpool, Ian was tragically killed in a car crash. That left both Wendy and me asking questions about the point of life.

So far, my weekly routine consisted of going to work all week so I could spend my wages on one night of pleasure, drinking, going to nightclubs, and trying to make some friends. I remember waking up one morning and being very sick because of all I had drunk the night before. It was as if I knew I was destroying my life, but I didn't care.

I worked for a few months in a cash and carry. After a few weeks I was called into the security manager's office. He accused me of stealing from the store. I wouldn't have minded, but I hadn't actually stolen anything there yet! He threatened me – then phoned for the police. They removed me from the store, in full view of staff and customers.

The police drove me to my bedsit where they tipped everything out on the floor, in search of stolen goods. They found nothing. Then they drove me to the police station and questioned me for a few hours about the things I was supposed to have stolen. They knew about my criminal record and said they knew I'd done something because things had been reported missing over a period of time. They assured me they were going to keep a close watch over me.

When I returned to the store, the staff made it clear that they didn't trust me any more. So I left. Soon afterwards I began a new job as a delivery driver for a laundry company – and heard that the security officer and manager at my previous place of employment had been arrested and convicted of theft and fraud.

Still, that didn't take away from the fact that I had lost a good friend, my family didn't want me, I couldn't keep a job for more than six months and my so-called friends had rejected me. I just didn't see any point to my life at all. As the weeks went by, I became more and more unhappy. Deep inside, I felt empty.

Every night I tried to untangle the mess I called 'my life'. One night I remember looking back on the whole series of disasters that formed the sum total of my existence so far. The dark realisation hit me. There was no one in the world who liked me.

'What's the point to it all?' I asked myself.

As I sat there, alone, I contemplated ending it all. It seemed the only thing that made sense. Did it really matter whether I lived another single day – or another fifty years? I wondered what was at the end of life. Was it just a black void? Was it heaven? Would I come back as something else? I had an idea that there must be something else after death. As a child, I'd become preoccupied with death and took pleasure in killing animals and birds. I would often visit the graveyard and wander around, thinking about death.

I was told about a meeting that a group of children were going to have in a nearby village hall. I didn't go. But I heard later that those kids – some no more than fourteen – had got hold of a Ouija board and had tried to use it. The windows of the hall smashed, and the children fled in fear of their lives. As I thought about this I became interested in the afterlife and the paranormal.

I bought a few books and read with interest stories of reincarnations, ghosts and other like things. The more I read the more I wanted these things to happen to me. I sought out ghost stories and went to places where ghosts had been spotted. Voices began to speak in my mind.

The more I thought, the more desperate I became. But the pain and loneliness were becoming too much to cope with. The voices in my head told me to do unspeakable things. Suicide seemed the only option.

I tried to do things to stop the voices. But I was also encouraging the voices by reading more books on the occult, or watching programmes on the occult or that were sexually explicit.

'Just look at it all,' I said to myself. 'What a mess.' I considered the various ways of taking my own life, when a different kind of idea popped into my mind.

'What if there is a God?' I thought.

I hadn't been to church for many years. In fact I had only ever been a couple of times. Once was with my school to sing one Christmas for the assembled parents. The other was when I went to the harvest supper at the local church because it was free grub for kids!

'Your mission,' my mother informed me, 'is to try to nick as much food as possible without being noticed.'

So I didn't have a very good grounding in the Christian faith! I thought it was all nonsense, actually. It was something that nice people did. The only churchgoers I knew of were the vicar and his family. On a couple of occasions they invited me to their home after school for tea. I remember him telling us stories of Noah and the

Ark. The fact that he fed me impressed me. I don't remember who he was or remember anyone else from the church. But there was this man who greeted me when I went into church and gave me a sweet.

I remember sitting at a small shelf, which served as my table in my room, and thinking, 'Does God care, does God exist?' So I thought I'd try and say a prayer and ask God if he was there. It must have been an amazing prayer – because I don't remember using any swear words at all.

I used to swear because everyone else I knew did. Bad language was just part of my day. I didn't think, 'I will now swear' – I just swore, mainly in between the words! My lifestyle was learned behaviour from others around me. I wanted desperately to fit in. So I did what everyone else did. At school the peer pressure was greatest. You either conformed or you stood out as a jerk. After school I just got into the habit of talking and living like that. So for me to pray at all, without swearing, was completely out of character! I don't know what made me do it, but the results of that prayer were to change my life dramatically, to say the least.

When I finished saying to God, 'Please help me,' he answered me. When I say he answered me, I mean he really did answer me. God audibly spoke to me. I could hear a voice that spoke to me. The voice said, 'I am with you.'

It wasn't like the other voices I'd been hearing. This one was an audible voice which came from behind me. And something inside me confirmed that it was God. It's hard to express. I can't remember the tone – just that it was gentle, but firm. And the moment the voice spoke to me, it filled me with excitement, not fear. It was the kind of voice that you know you have to obey. So I did!

The voice told me to go to Tunbridge Wells in Kent

and seek God there. Nothing else. No address. No directions. He just said, 'Go.' Since then, some people have asked me, 'Was it really a voice that spoke to you, or a feeling inside?' Well, I know for certain that night I heard an audible voice from heaven speak to me. It's hard to explain. It actually happened. It was real. I was feeling very excited. I just couldn't sleep. When I woke the following morning I felt somewhat different. I remembered what had taken place the night before.

'I've got to leave here, and go to Tunbridge Wells,' I said to myself.

So I gave in my two weeks' notice. I sold everything I had. That included a radio and a Sinclair computer! Then I left to search for God. My wonderful bedsit sale had raised just enough to get me to Tunbridge Wells – with a little left over.

It was September 1981 when I arrived in Tunbridge Wells. As a family, we'd lived about ten miles west of the town. I remembered one or two shops – that was all. I didn't have a clue why I was going, where I would live, or anything. All I knew was that God had spoken to me. And I had to obey. I took a train. It seemed a very long trip, and I was expecting something to happen and wanted to get on with a new life. As each station went past my window, the more expectant I became.

On arriving there, I wandered around waiting for God to speak to me again and show me what he wanted. But there was silence. I felt alone again. Was it just a dream – or did it really happen the way I'd remembered it?

I knew I had to think quickly, and so found an advertisement for a bedsit. I phoned, and a woman offered me the room. She agreed to meet me one hour later. I stood outside the newsagent's, where I had found the advertisement, waiting for the lady to show up. All sorts of voices started shouting in my mind – voices that seemed only to want harm, not good, to come into my life.

Then someone approached me. It was the woman I'd talked with on the phone. She introduced herself and her husband. They were short and elderly, with grey hair and furry coats. They both smiled at me and invited me across the road to view the bedsit. As we walked into the house I felt cold. It seemed warmer outside than in. We walked up the dimly lit stairs, and I felt gloomy. But I knew that if this was the place God wanted for me, then he would show me what to do.

I was shown the shared bathroom. Then we walked to the next floor where my bedsit was. It was just big enough for a bed and a small chest of drawers. At the end of my bed was a tiny sink and the window which overlooked the road below.

The couple told me that the lady in the next bedsit was a bit eccentric. 'Just ignore her,' they said. Her name was Doris. She would wander the streets every day collecting rubbish, which she dragged up the stairs and into her room.

Later, I came home one evening to find her door open and saw that she was leaning against a set of drawers – fast asleep! Around her were piles of rubbish – mainly cardboard – all stacked in neat piles. Some of the floorboards had been taken up and she'd filled the holes with soil where she was growing plants! What a girl.

A few weeks later I bought a little black and white TV. I wanted to connect the aerial, so I opened the skylight in the bathroom and climbed out on to the roof to find a connection. After I'd connected it, the heavens opened and it began to rain. So I went to climb back through the skylight only to find Doris sitting in the bath having a wash. Fortunately, she was still fully clothed! The people in the street must have wondered why I was sitting on the roof in the rain. Eventually I got back in.

Next on my list of priorities was to find work. I wandered up to the job centre only to be informed – after I explained that I'd just come from the north – that there were no jobs at that moment. As I looked around the bright walls of the centre, each advertisement hammered home the fact that I had no qualifications whatsoever.

It seemed hopeless. Then I began to wander around the town centre. I found myself in a large department store looking at things for my bedsit. It wasn't as if I could afford anything. After paying for one week's rent I was left with about three pounds for the week!

'Hello,' someone said. I took no notice as I thought this friendly greeting must be for someone else. I heard someone speak a second time, and this time I knew he was greeting me. I looked up and saw a young man. I responded, and we began to talk. Within minutes the man said to me, 'You don't want a job, do you?'

I couldn't believe my ears. I accepted the job and was asked to begin the next day. It was as if it was all planned. The man turned out to be the store manager. The job was a salesman in the silverware department. My role was to sell the gear and to keep polishing all the shelves and the silver.

More amazing things happened that week. I stopped swearing and stealing. It was just as though something – or someone – had taken those desires away from me. Now all I wanted to do was to find out more about this God who was answering my prayers. Church immediately came into my mind.

'That's it,' I concluded, 'if I want to find God I'll have to go to a church. That's where God lives. That's God's gaff!' It seemed such a simple idea. Go to church. Talk to God. Say thanks for a new start.

As I woke on the Sunday morning the same thought came into my head: 'Go to church.' So I left my room, went out into the street and began to look for a church. I didn't need to look very far. There at the bottom of the road, just around the corner, was a church. I looked up at the grey building and wondered what it would be like on the inside.

I was early. The service wasn't due to start for another half an hour. But I walked up the steps of the building and was greeted by a big man with a big smile who gave me a pile of books.

'He must want something, with a grin like that,' I thought.

Maybe I had to pay for the books on the way out or something. So I became rather preoccupied with the books. But when everyone else arrived they all seemed to have them. So maybe it was all right. Everyone looked posh. They'd all dressed up for church. I stuck out like a lion in a den of Daniels.

Some of the people – two ladies especially – thought I was going to rob them. But they began to pray for me. It was obvious they were middle class. But that didn't enter my mind. I was just amazed that people would want to come to a dusty building like this each week.

I sat down at the front of the church. A woman came and sat next to me. She asked me my name and where I lived. I was a little hesitant giving out that type of information. So I said something that I thought would please her. In the past, people who asked me questions were usually the police. I wasn't expecting all the questions – and had some fears that she might actually be the police. If you're streetwise, you just don't go around giving out your personal details.

Then she left and the service began. A man in a dress told us all what to do next. Then a choir marched in, singing. I was surprised by the fact that there were some young people and children there. The children went out somewhere at the beginning of the service. I was amazed by the way the people sang – as if they really believed what they were singing. I wondered what the catch was, as most people seemed to be enjoying themselves.

It was good to be able to sing. I hadn't done that for a long time. If for nothing else, I decided I would come back the next Sunday for a good sing. But God had other plans, as I was to find out. The same woman who'd talked to me before the service began came and spoke to me again. This time she invited me to lunch.

As soon as she said the word 'lunch', the word 'yes' just came out of my mouth even before I could think. 'Good,' was her reply. She invited me to walk with her to her house which, she informed me, was just through the park at the back of church. When I went up the driveway of her house I looked at the sign on the entrance. It said 'Vicarage'. It turned out this woman was the vicar's wife!

The vicarage was large with no carpets, just polished floors and rugs. It was warm inside, and there was a wonderful smell of cooking as we walked in through the front door. For the first fifteen minutes there was just me and the vicar's wife. She took me into the kitchen, complaining about her back being bad.

'Do you mind if I lie down on the floor?' she asked me, getting ready to hit the deck.

'Of course I don't – it's your house,' I said.

'Be a dear and take the potatoes out of the oven and put the veg on,' she continued, motioning from her new horizontal position. And I was the guest!

Soon afterwards the vicar arrived and took over, stepping over his wife on the floor. The house smelled of food and polish. All was quiet except for a clock constantly ticking in the hall. The autumn was upon us and the trees in the garden were turning brown. It was a lovely setting. The couple had three children. Two were present for lunch. Their son was about fifteen, so we got on quite well. They seemed very nice.

Now I was stuck and began to feel very uncomfortable. It was a good lunch, and I appreciated being accepted into the home of someone who didn't know me at all. After the meal I was invited to join the family on a walk. On returning to the vicarage I was asked to have a cup of tea with them. Then, later in the afternoon, the lady asked if I'd like to go with them to church. 'What again?' I replied. I didn't know that people would want to go twice in one day. But to be polite I said yes – and went to church with them.

After the service someone invited me to a Bible study group on the Wednesday. 'A what?' I replied, 'What do you do there?' The person explained that a small group of them met together to pray, read the Bible and then enjoy something they called fellowship. That included food. So I was in.

That Wednesday, it was another lovely evening as I wandered through the park to the address I'd been given. I remember trying to find the house, which was just up the road from where I was living. It was set back in a little unmade road. It was just getting dark when I rang the doorbell. A lady called Joyce came to the door. I was one of the first there. I was invited in and sat down in the sitting room.

All the chairs were placed in a large circle around the room. Gradually the room filled up. Someone said a prayer then read from the Bible. All the people began to chat about what they thought it meant and then sang a short song. There were no hymnbooks in sight.

Then the group prayed about certain people and for a place in Africa where one day they hoped to build a hospital. The guy who had welcomed me at church on the Sunday was there – as were a couple of people from the choir. They had something that I didn't have and enjoyed being together, taking an interest in each other's activities during the week. I found the praying-and-reading-the-Bible bits hard work. So I was glad when the refreshments arrived. It was a good evening.

'I like these Christians,' I thought. I enjoyed their company and appreciated the food. I think I was hooked.

2

School for a Scoundrel

I turned off the TV, knelt down in front of the screen and wept. I had previously listened but never understood. Now what was locked away in my mind had come into focus. I experienced an amazing feeling of love inside. I knew I had to accept the fact that God loved me. I had forgotten how to cry. I had always been told by my mum how crying was stupid – especially for a boy. So I had stopped any tears, and hadn't cried for many years.

Now I couldn't hold back. I looked back on my life. I felt so bad about all that I had done – the houses I had broken into, the people I had stolen from, the language I had used, the films I had seen. The list just went on and on. Then, in my mind, I saw Jesus and felt forgiven. I gave my life to God the only way I knew. I said thank you and asked that he would now take charge of my life – and lead me to do good things and not bad. And all because I'd sat and watched *Ben Hur* on the telly one Sunday afternoon!

Of course, there had been a build-up to that point. Attending Christchurch in Tunbridge Wells was a major turning point. It seemed amazing. I had actually found a group of people who really were excited about God. And they meant it.

Here was a group of people who had something that I was looking for. They had a joy and a peace about them that I wanted in my life. But how could I get it? How could I become like them? I was hooked. But hooked on to what? Something was happening inside me again. Something I could feel, something that was directing me to seek, look and find.

'Why not give it another Sunday?' I thought. 'Perhaps God will speak to me again, like he did in Blackpool, and show me what to do.'

All I wanted to do was to say thanks to God for helping me out. I also wanted to revisit these new friends I had met the previous Wednesday.

Sunday morning came round soon enough. As the sun shone through my window on that bright September morning, I could think of nothing else but church, God and these wonderful people I had met. I dressed and went out into the street, feeling excited but apprehensive.

'Will church be the same this week or were those people putting it all on?' I thought. I also asked myself, 'Am I really feeling this and doing this?'

It wasn't like a dream. But I did feel as if I had woken up from one. I was touching on a new reality. It felt too good to be true, but at the same time I knew it was true. My previous life – though I didn't start to see it like that at the time – was becoming so unreal that now I felt that I was doing something I had been designed for. I fitted in.

It only took me about three minutes to walk the short distance between my bedsit and the church. I arrived early and received the same welcome as I had the previous week. This time the man remembered my name! Each Sunday I went to church and each Wednesday to Bible study. I was learning new things about God, who he was and that he loved us all. I heard all sorts of stuff about Jesus and the Bible. At other times they would talk about the Holy Spirit. It was all information that my mind had never taken in before. And I liked what I heard.

Most of the people in the church were elderly. But the generation gap didn't matter much to me. I wouldn't say at that stage they were friends, but I saw in them something of family. And it felt great to be around older people who didn't want to beat me or abuse me, but just to enjoy my company – and I enjoyed theirs. The church had a youth leader, Marilyn. I soon got to know her and some of the youth group.

What puzzled me the most was this guy Jesus. It seemed to me that he was a pretty amazing person – doing miracles and things like that. But then to allow himself to die for no crime of his own didn't make any sense at all. I knew that Jesus rose again after he died. We sang about it every Sunday. So why did he die in the first place, I wondered? Wouldn't it have been easier just to stay alive? Wouldn't it have been far less hassle and pain?

After church one Sunday morning, I went back to my bedsit and watched TV. By that time I'd managed to purchase a few things for the room. And after my camping cooker, the top item of luxury was this little black and white set. It was raining outside. And the only thing I felt like doing, after enjoying a full Sunday lunch of beans on toast, was to watch something on the box.

While the trains thundered beneath me – my bedsit was just 150 yards from the main station – I sat down to see what was on BBC 1. After all, it was the only channel I received that didn't have interference on it. And that's when I tuned into *Ben Hur*. I don't know why the film itself attracted me. I just know that I couldn't believe it went on for so long. I enjoyed the story. But I was intrigued to see a short sequence devoted to telling the story about this guy Jesus, who I'd heard about in church.

In the movie, Jesus was portrayed as someone very special who healed people and gave hope to those who had no hope. A couple of scenes referred to him. The first was the part where Ben Hur is taken captive and is walking along the road chained to hundreds of other criminals. The Roman soldiers allow the prisoners to stop for water. But they make sure no one gives Ben Hur anything to drink. Then, while one of the soldiers isn't looking, a figure appears and his shadow falls over the face of Ben Hur.

The man gives Ben Hur a drink, much to the annoyance of the guard, who by this time has spun around and noticed the man's kind act. The soldier approaches the man shouting, and with anger he draws back his hand ready to strike. Then the soldier looks at his face, which is hidden from the camera, and his own face pales. Fear comes over the soldier. He turns and walks away. The man is Jesus.

There was just something about him that made people see things from a different perspective. The memory of that scene remains with me to this day. What struck me most was how a man could have control over another person without having to say or do anything. Jesus' divinity shone through in that clip. I wanted to find out who this man was, because it wasn't completely obvious at that point in the film. Who was this guy who had such power? I was drawn to him.

The second part of the film that I remember being pivotal in my understanding of who Jesus was and why he died was the sequence when Jesus was being made to carry his cross and then was nailed upon it. The charge that was placed over his head was the reason for his crucifixion. It said, 'The King of the Jews'. It wasn't until many years later that I fully realised that here was a man who had been killed not for what he had done – like the two thieves by his side – but for who he was.

When I saw Jesus dying on a cross, all sorts of things began to flood into my mind – things I had heard in church and Bible study about Jesus dying in my place. Everything I had heard about in church came together, rather like pieces of a jigsaw. I understood, for the first time, that God loved me. God actually felt good about me and loved me so much that he was prepared to let his own son suffer and die in my place. I knew I was bad inside, and understood that if you ever did wrong you were punished. That was something I'd learned from early childhood – you do something wrong and you get walloped. So I knew that God would have to punish me for all the bad things I had ever done in my life – things the Bible calls 'sin'.

I needed and wanted to be forgiven. But what I didn't know was that God wanted to forgive me. Me – a burglar, a horrible person! God wanted to forgive me for all the bad that was in my life. All I needed to do was to accept it. So I did. I'd come to realise that, instead of punishing me for all the wrong I'd ever done, he punished his own son in my place. That was truly amazing. Then I understood why Jesus had to die. *Ben Hur* helped trigger all those thoughts. And that had led to my point of confession – in front of the TV!

The next morning the sun shone brightly through my curtains. I awoke. As I lay there, for a few moments all the thoughts and feelings of the previous day came flooding through my mind. Quickly, I dressed for work. I noticed that I felt very different inside. It was as if someone had given me a thorough cleaning while I slept. I felt so joyful inside, and was looking forward to going to work and telling everyone what had happened.

As I left the house, I couldn't believe what I saw. The late September day was bright and warm. The flowers, trees, the sky – in fact everything around me – seemed different. It felt as if someone had taken a layer of grey off my eyes and unblocked my ears. I heard the birds singing. I wondered why I had never heard them sing so beautifully before. Why was it that the flowers seemed so much brighter than I had ever noticed previously?

Walking past the park, as I did every day, now became an experience of beauty and colour as the autumn trees swayed in the breeze. Even now, looking back on that day, I can still feel some of those very same feelings – feelings of newness and knowing that something once and for all had changed, deep inside me. I sang some hymns on the walk to work, receiving some funny looks from those standing at bus stops or passing me by on the road. I had a tremendous joy in my heart. And I wanted the whole world to know.

My friends at work really weren't interested in hearing what had happened. But I told them anyway! At the end of the day I rushed home so I could read the Bible, which I found helped me understand God more. I soon got bogged down and felt like giving up. I knew the Bible was exciting, as we had examined it every week at Bible study. But the bit I was reading was just lists of names which I didn't understand. I decided to seek the advice of a wise Christian friend who asked me what book in the Bible I was studying. I showed her that I had begun in Genesis and was now in Numbers. My hunger for God's message meant that I was reading it whenever and wherever I could.

'Try reading the new bit,' my friend told me.

'New bit?' I exclaimed. 'It's all new – I've just bought it!'

'No,' she said, 'the New Testament.' And she went on to explain that the first four books of the New Testament were about Jesus and his miracles. So I was given 'permission' to jump loads of books and began reading from Matthew's account of Jesus. As I started to read the Bible I wondered how to do all the things that Jesus did – especially since he told his disciples that they would do greater things than he had done.

I read the bit about how important Jesus said it was for us to tell other people about him. After reading that, I knew I just had to go out there, on the streets, and tell people about Jesus. So one afternoon I went out and just began talking to people about Jesus, much to the astonishment of many – even some from the church! I remember talking to some of the people in church one evening about how important it was for us all to get out and tell everyone that God loves them. I explained how I had been doing that, and thought others would like to join me.

'We don't do it like that here,' someone said.

I wanted to shout out loud from the rooftops that Jesus was alive. But I felt as if I was the only one like that! I remember reading one day about Jesus healing someone. Then I heard about a man who was very ill in hospital. So I prayed. It was incredible. The man got better!

I learned so much from my friends at Christchurch, Tunbridge Wells. They were very patient and loving with me. They encouraged me when I was down, taught me how to love and serve God – and showed me how I was going to be used by God for greater things than selling silverware.

One dear lady from the church recently told me how she remembered the day I arrived at Christchurch. Apparently I had seemed very threatening to the elderly people there. Many of them were afraid of me. They thought I would steal their handbags or something. But one lady believed that God could actually change the heart of this rebel – and so began to pray for me. I thank God for people like Molly who trusted in Jesus and faithfully prayed for the impossible.

Something had happened to me. And I was keen to tell everyone. My family seemed to greet the news of my transformation with as much joy as they greeted the arrival of the dustman. Yet I began to tell others. I tried to spend time telling people what joy I had found. So I began to go out on to the streets on a Saturday and tell others what God had done for me. I also started a club in the church hall for children who didn't know much of God.

I didn't realise that I was supposed to get all sorts of things agreed by a church council, talk to the youth worker, arrange a meeting and pray for 'God's guidance'. I just did it and learned much on the way. Looking back, I'm so thankful that the church and the youth leader were patient with me and encouraged my new zeal for God, while trying to direct me into more edifying evangelistic events than a Hallowe'en party! Fortunately, the youth leader intercepted our party plan before it happened, explaining that the church disapproved of celebrating Hallowe'en. But I'd already begun to arrange some fund-raising for the youth club by doing 'trick or treat' around people's houses and asking for donations!

As the youth club grew in numbers, many others became involved and helped me in my new work. Some of the young people started to ask me all sorts of questions about God and the Bible. I realised I knew very little indeed. My youth worker helped where she could. She felt that God was calling me to go to Bible college to serve him full-time.

What an idea – Bible college! That was actually the last place on earth I was thinking of going. So I continued in my work with the children and young people. My idea was this: I didn't want the children and young people getting into the same mess as I had previously. Whatever I could do to guide them towards Jesus was, for me, a great way of saying thank you to God.

It was a sad Sunday when the vicar informed us all in the church service that he, his wife and family were being called to another parish. A few months later they had left, and the church welcomed the new vicar, Rev. John Banner and his family, from Liverpool. But I was soon encouraged as I realised how serious this new vicar was about God. He seemed willing to spend time teaching me some wonderful things about God and how to share that knowledge practically with others. I grew to love John and his family as they took me into their home and welcomed me as one of their own. For the first time in my life I realised that someone actually loved me, somebody wanted to care – and was prepared to show it.

John enrolled me in courses for discipleship and evangelism. All the time I was fighting against the wise counsel of my youth worker to go to Bible college. I was part of the youth group, but, at twenty-two, an elderly member. Yet no one seemed to bother. We all just got on so well.

The youth group was split into two age sections – fourteen- to sixteen-year-olds and eighteen plus – but we all did things together. I was part of the second group, but enjoyed being with the teenagers. One girl took my fancy and we did go out for a while. She was my first real long-term girlfriend. But some said she was just a bit young for me, at fifteen.

Then one day, as I was praying, I really felt God wanted me to go to Bible college. I can't explain how or why I felt what I did. It was just one of those things – like moving from Blackpool to Tunbridge Wells. I knew God wanted me to do it. I convinced myself more and more that it was what God wanted. By that time, the voice of God had become so distinct that every other sound was just noise in comparison. At first I had struggled to accept going to Bible college. I thought it would be full of religious people, so I hadn't been too keen at the start. Now that view was changing.

The more I prayed about it, the more it seemed right to me. I asked God daily about this matter, as it was a big step for me to take. My fears and earlier rejection of the idea of going to Bible college were based on the idea that it was a 'holy' place where people studied all day long. The thought of spending a couple of years with all those holy people filled me with fear.

My friend and youth worker, Marilyn, encouraged me to write away and apply to various Bible colleges, and maybe visit a couple of them. Then I could see for myself that they were inhabited by 'normal' people! I wasn't convinced. But I wrote to them anyway – just to keep her off my back.

A week went by. I hadn't heard from any of the colleges. I actually told Marilyn that God didn't want me to go as I had heard nothing. She encouraged me to pray, and trust God to lead me. I did, and as I prayed I said to God that if I didn't hear from a college by Monday morning, then I would know he didn't want me to go there.

Guess what arrived on my doorstep that Monday morning! Yes, a letter from Moorlands College with information and an application form to apply for entrance. 'Okay, God,' I thought, 'if this is of you then I will go.' As I read through the literature, it scared me to think of all the academic work people had to do.

I hadn't been a bright student. I hated school and didn't

see any point in studying or reading books about things that were so totally irrelevant to my life at the time. My teachers had categorised me as 'too disruptive', and so I was given jobs to do around school instead of going to lessons. I thought that getting the cane was bad enough. But having to pick up litter or do gardening around school was even worse. One of the two exams I sat resulted in failure because the class rioted. We used to throw paper and chairs around the room – one young female teacher had fled from the room, crying.

So I knew I could never study, especially something full-time. But I sent off my application anyway. The only part I wasn't sure of was the page where you had to list the books you had read recently, and then the ones that had affected your life in some way – and why. However, the only book I had ever read all the way through was *The Wizard Of Oz*! I wrote that down anyway, hoping they wouldn't notice. Moorlands College replied a week or so later and invited me to go for an interview. Amazing as it seemed at the time, they appeared to be interested.

The day of the interview came: it was June 1984. I made my way to Dorset and arrived for the grilling. I was scared stiff going there, but soon felt very much at home. The academic side was worrying me. I had my interview in the morning after chapel and after being invited to sit in on one of the first-year lectures. The interview room was quiet. My palms were saturated with sweat. My heart jumped when two lecturers came into the room – Stuart Pascall and Brian Butler. One asked me all about my spiritual life and how I had become a Christian. The other asked me about what plans I had to serve God and how I thought I was going to pay for my fees each term. Strangely enough, they didn't ask me the spiritual significance of *The Wizard Of Oz*!

I tried to answer their questions as best I could. When it came to the finance bit, I just explained that I had no money whatsoever, but knew that if God wanted me at Bible college, he would provide. I could see them look at each other as if to say, 'Well, we'd better not reply to that one.' I returned home and waited for a reply. A few days later a letter arrived from the college offering me a place! In September 1984 I began my three-year course of biblical studies.

There was so much to learn. I felt that I wasn't going to cope with all this academic stuff! There were books to read, lectures to go to and papers to write. The good news was that there were some rather interesting opportunities to be a Christian and serve God through missions and helping churches tell people about Jesus. I learned very early on what it was to trust God. I went with £500 in the bank. Knowing that the fees were £500 per term, I had to trust that if this was the place God wanted me to be, then he would have to provide all I needed. And sure enough, he did.

The first thing I noticed was that as I prayed, things would happen – not just in my life, but also in the lives of others. God began to show me what it meant practically to have 'faith'. My first year had gone well – even though I had struggled with many of the papers and trying to cope with learning all over again. It was in my second year that I began to learn that God really could be trusted with everything. All through the first year God had provided through other Christians. And the timing was always so spot on.

In my second term of the second year, I was completely broke. I didn't even have enough money for a postage stamp, so I couldn't write to anyone and ask for money. It was on the last night of term that I became desperate. I was sitting in my room, which I shared with a godly man called Simon Lang, and was going through my finances. As I added up my sums, I realised I was £200 short of paying my fees for that term. How could I have overlooked such a thing? I knew I'd better have the money by the next morning – or I was in trouble. So I began to pray. I had no one else to turn to who could help.

After a short time of prayer there was a knock at the door of my room. It couldn't have been Simon, I thought: he was in the student lounge. And I wasn't expecting any visitors as it was nearly 10.00 p.m. As I opened the door, my caller turned out to be a man who'd driven over from Bournemouth because he knew, as he explained later, that he needed to see me. 'I saw you in church on Sunday,' he said, 'and I was thinking about you this evening when my wife and I were discussing some insurance money that we had received this week. I don't know anything about you really – or what your needs are. But we really feel that God wants us to give this money to you.' He handed me an envelope and then left. As soon as the door had closed, I ripped open the envelope – to find £200 inside!

On returning to Tunbridge Wells for my Easter break I found out that a young Australian lady, Jenni, was visiting England and was staying in town. She was the talk of the young men of the church – all three of us! I met her on the Sunday and was very impressed by her. I loved the look of her – she seemed sporty, which I liked, she was chatty and attractive. She was always talking about God and obviously had a love for him. I knew I had to see her again and couldn't stop thinking about her and what she looked like.

She told me she had a found a job locally in a sports shop. The following day I decided to check out things for myself and make a visit to the store. As I walked up to the town I became increasingly aware of my own footwear. I didn't have the most trendy trainers in the world – and they were ripped across the front. When I walked, the trainers would flap around and when it rained they would let water in. I had taped them up to stop the flapping noise, but knew that I was in need of a new pair.

The shop was large and certainly had an air of fitness about it. Then, through the tennis racquets, I spotted her. After some small talk, Jenni asked me about my trainers. Well, they were rather embarrassing – with both shoes split around the toes and one kept together with parcel tape. A few minutes later Jenni had found me a pair of trainers on special offer for £20. I explained that I hadn't got the money to purchase them. She encouraged me to pray and ask God for the money. I was the one from Bible college – and she was telling me to pray to God about my needs!

Later, I invited Jenni to the cinema – supposedly with the rest of the youth group. When she met me outside, she asked me where all the others were. I explained that they couldn't come, which was code for 'I haven't invited them – only you.' I walked her home afterwards and it was just love from then on. We arranged to see each other at the youth group and things progressed nicely from there.

While returning to the vicar's house from the sports shop, I prayed. When I arrived, he said one of the ladies from the church had called while I was out and was desperate to see me. He drove me over to her house in Frant, a small village near Tunbridge Wells. Sybil opened the door, invited me in and told me to go through to the lounge and sit down. I sat down and was encouraged to see a coffee table with a small shelf underneath. It proved to be a great hiding place for my smelly trainers! Over a cup of tea Sybil explained that as she was praying that morning, God had spoken to her and told her something about me. I was keen to find out exactly what.

'God told me to give you this,' she said as she handed me an envelope, 'it's for footwear!' You can imagine what I felt when I opened the envelope and found two £10 notes inside. God is so faithful. He was teaching me so much about putting my life in his hands.

After the Easter break it was back to college and back to all this stuff like New Testament studies, Greek and learning the difference between a verb and a noun. Even English was foreign to me! It was a busy term. My friend and room-mate Simon Lang and I had begun to plan a trip to Poland.

Two Polish students had begun to study at Moorlands while I was in my second year. They told us stories of their country, their church and their struggle. I must admit to not being very interested. I had never been interested in anything outside the UK. I also knew that God would never call me overseas. When I went to Moorlands I'd told God that I would do anything for him – so long as it wasn't overseas or in a city. I often think back to that 'deal' I made with God, especially years later when he called me to work in a city overseas!

Poland wasn't a place I had planned to spend my summer vacation. But when Simon and I heard about those who were suffering, we decided we couldn't sit back and let this happen. We needed to do something. Without much thought, we planned a summer trip to Poland. The plan was that we'd drive the two Polish students back to Warsaw, taking with us some supplies for the church there.

As the weeks went by, the list of things needed in Poland grew. We prayed and trusted that God would help us to find the money and equipment needed for the trip. It was amazing to see the way fellow students and local churches became interested and involved in the scheme. A short time later a whole new idea had begun to emerge in our minds – a larger mission project to Poland.

It hadn't begun that way. But the mission to Poland project really took off. With donated funds we bought a long-wheel-base Land Rover. High on the list of priority items was a large quantity of medical supplies. We'd made contact with an organisation that could let us have all we needed for a great price. And since we didn't have the money to pay on delivery, the college loaned it to us – with the understanding that it was all paid back the day the college term finished. Simon and I signed a piece of paper to assure the college that it would be paid.

I remember thinking back to the time when I needed £200 for my fees and how God had answered that need. If God had provided then, I mused, God could and would provide for us now. As the weeks flew by and spring turned into summer, money was arriving at the college for the medical supplies, as well as for all the other things we were planning on buying once the college had been repaid.

One evening Simon, the two Polish students, some others and I met together to pray about the forthcoming trip. One thing was on our minds: the £900 needed by the next morning, the day college finished for the summer. I had a strong feeling that God wanted us to go and pray in the Land Rover and to trust him to provide our needs. Everyone thought it was a mad idea. So off we went.

Towards the end of the prayer meeting I had such a feeling of trust that God would certainly provide the £900 needed. By that time it was dark and the early summer evening was cool. I encouraged our prayer group to return inside and just praise God for his sure and certain provision. As we came back into the main building, I looked in my post box. There was an envelope in it. I collected it and took it upstairs where we were going to meet to praise God. On opening the envelope I found a cheque inside for £800! Even though everyone was praising God for the money, my thoughts turned to the other £100 that was needed. So we continued to pray and trust God, and in the next morning's post was a cheque for £200. God spoke to my heart again about his faithfulness and how he could be trusted in all things.

So with a Land Rover full of medical equipment, Bibles, teaching materials and food, the four of us set off for Poland. God had provided all we needed and had given us £100 extra, which we took with us. We didn't know it at the time, but we had calculated wrongly about the cost of the ferry. The extra sum of money needed at Dover came to almost £100.

I had learned so much from my new relationship with God. And there were many other lessons I had to learn – especially regarding my British arrogance and pride.

Our drive to Warsaw was a long one, two days in all. At times the beauty of the countryside was quite breathtaking. On the night we arrived in Warsaw, we were invited to a meal in the basement of the church. What impressed me most was the wonderful spread of food that had been laid on for us by one of the families of the church.

After eating my fill, the thought came to me about how real the poverty there was. How was it that this family could provide so much food if they were so poor? Maybe they weren't poor after all, and this was just a ploy to get some Western supplies to their country. The thought filled me with rage as I told the two Polish students what I thought of the situation.

'How come,' I asked, 'that this family can afford all

this food if they are so poor?' I was about to receive a revelation.

'You probably don't realise it,' said one of the Polish students, 'but you've just eaten their week's food supply!' Their reply shocked and humbled me so much, I vowed to never again judge a situation only by what I could see.

We were taken to Auschwitz to see the old concentration camps. I felt quite ill from the trip. But the whole experience made me realise again what was really important in life. As we looked around the camps and walked into the gas chambers I could feel cries of pain from within me – cries that called for justice. The whole place was silent.

The piles of glasses, false teeth, suitcases and hair were evidence that something very wrong had happened, but at least something had been done to bring it to an end. What about those people who were still suffering great injustices around the world, I thought. Later that day I met a survivor of the Holocaust. I looked into his eyes and saw how the inexpressible pain had been replaced by Jesus' love.

Poland was the first time I saw real poverty. God showed me other people's pain in a way that I had never experienced before. I realised that I wasn't the only one who had suffered – and now I could help others know his love. The Polish people looked as if they had given up on life. They had tried and life had failed them, and now all they could do was sit it out. Some escaped by taking drugs or drinking alcohol. There was no hope for a better future – they just went through the motions.

Returning to college after the summer break was like seeing the world through new eyes. The passages in the Bible about the poor and needy seemed to have a new meaning. God had begun a new work in my life as I began to reassess my priorities and decided to live a simpler lifestyle. As one person put it, I wanted to live simply so that others could simply live.

With that in mind, I found the suggestion of having a car hard to comprehend. I had been working with a boys' group at a church in Christchurch, Bournemouth, for one year. The weekly trip into town was becoming harder on a bicycle, especially with all the things I was trying to take with me. My friend Simon Lang suggested that I pray and ask God for a car. At first I didn't give it much thought, because I couldn't get used to the idea of asking God for something that big. But after a few days of thinking further on the issue, I decided that I might ask God for a car. So I asked Simon to pray with me.

Simon suggested that we be specific in asking God for a car, and ask him for what I really wanted. 'What type of car do you want to ask God for?' he said to me. I thought it was a joke. But Simon didn't seem to be joking. I didn't know much about cars, so I decided just to ask God for a red one. I told Simon not to tell anyone that we were praying about the car as I felt rather embarrassed about it.

About a week went by. I was working in the college kitchens when a student walked in and asked to speak to me. His name was Tim. He felt that he needed to talk to me urgently. He began by saying that he thought God wanted him to buy me a car; did I need one? At that point I didn't think to myself, 'Praise the Lord!' I actually thought that Simon had sent him to me to wind me up.

As that thought crossed my mind, the only feeling that hit me was rage! I grabbed Tim by the shirt and threw him through the swing doors between the kitchen and dining room. As Tim landed in the dining room, I stood over him complaining about the 'wind-up' and telling him in no uncertain words what I thought of him. 'I don't understand,' he said, 'I didn't know you were praying about a car!' How I wished that the Second Coming had happened at that very moment.

Tim very graciously explained his story. That morning he had received £600 to cover his college fees in his post. In the next envelope he opened he found another cheque for £600. Apparently he had thought about why God would send him two lots of £600. As he pondered on that, I had passed by his window on my way into the main block. Tim thought and prayed about the money – and felt God telling him to give me the money for a car.

I felt such a fool and wished I had taken his news a little more seriously at the start. I explained to Tim that Simon and I had been praying for a couple of weeks for a red car and that I would show him what I bought when I found something. I then rushed off to find Simon and explained to him what had happened. He suggested he phone one of the members of his church in Blandford who was a mechanic and bought and sold cars now and again. He returned a few minutes later and said that his friend had a car for sale. In fact, it had only come in the previous day.

As we drove along the road towards Blandford that afternoon, I asked Simon what make of car it was. 'I don't know,' he said. He didn't even know what it cost or what colour it was. When we arrived at his friend's garage about thirty minutes later, there was one car sitting outside for sale. It was a red Avenger – for £600!

I was coming to realise that God is so real and is interested in all of my dreams. He has promised never to leave me alone and to walk through this life with me. I still find it hard to understand why God wants to use even me and why he desires to hear and answer my prayers.

By this time Jen had started working for the Church Pastoral Aid Society (CPAS) as their conference organiser.

She was travelling around the UK a lot, and was able to come and visit me at college on a couple of occasions. She was given one of the guest rooms and we spent time praying for each other and about the plans God had for us. When we weren't together we would write lengthy letters talking of how much God was doing in our lives, praying for each other and sharing Bible verses that God had challenged us with.

Jen came to college one weekend. It was over Hallowe'en and a group of students had left the campus to go and pray in a small village called Burley. Apparently there had been witchcraft there years ago and it was now a tourist attraction. So the students wanted to pray for peace and that God's love and power would be the attraction, not witchcraft. Jen and I spent hours talking together and then praying for each other. When it was late, Jen left for her room and I for mine.

She told me later that as she lay in bed, she was aware of someone else in the room. So she sat up. The room was dark but with enough light from the moon to highlight the shapes of the furniture. As she sat up she saw a dark figure standing at the bottom of her bed. It just stood there, and as Jen prayed for the protection of Jesus, the figure left. The experience made us both aware of the spiritual battle we were in as Christians, one we knew would not get easier but one we would always win in the name that is above every name.

During my final few days of Bible college, I believe that God continued to speak to me about all he wanted to do through me with children and young people. My relationship with Jen had grown over that year. It had grown so much that I asked her to marry me. I told her that I believed it was God's will for our lives to be together and serve him. She agreed. I was excited about getting married and working 'full-time' for God.

The day before college finished, the road tax ran out on my car. I was left wondering if God really would mind me driving a car that was just one day out of date with its tax. But I knew it was wrong. So I prayed and asked God for the £55 needed for the tax disc. The day college actually finished, I prayed even more for the money and trusted God to provide as he had done in the past. When the post arrived, I was keen to see what there was for me. One letter arrived with a cheque inside for £18. I praised God for his provision and asked him to provide the remainder – £37.

I was a little concerned. What was I to do? I loaded up the car with all my belongings and went to the final lunch, speeches, presentations and goodbyes. When I went to hand in my key to my room, the students were being told to go and check once more to make certain that we hadn't left anything behind. The college had boxes full of things that had been left by previous students.

I knew I had checked my room thoroughly, and that there was nothing in it apart from dust. But I checked it again anyway. As I went into this room that I hadn't planned to see ever again, there on the desk was £37 in cash! I was humbled before God. As I left college I was able to buy my tax disc from a post office in Ringwood before returning home to Tunbridge Wells.

Jen and I were busy preparing for our wedding day. By that time it was only two weeks away. We planned to travel to Australia the day after our wedding, to spend time with Jen's family and enjoy a honeymoon. We had just two weeks to prepare everything, and needed to sell the car to raise some money. We put an advertisement in the local paper, which came out two days before the wedding. We prayed and asked God to send a buyer for the car.

The evening the paper came out, we prayed again and asked God to send us one person that evening who would buy the car for cash. We had one phone call from a man who came around straight away. He looked at the car and said, 'OK, I'll take it for £600.'

3

The Second Miracle Child

'Jack,' the lady called, pointing to an elderly man in the congregation, 'come up here – God wants you to receive a blessing today.' So Jack went forward for prayer. Then he fell over!

There were always two church bodyguards at hand to catch anyone who reacted to prayer in that way. Just like our acquaintance with prophecy, we had heard about this phenomena happening to others and had even seen it. But we were rather sceptical.

'Weren't these people putting it all on?' we thought. 'Could it be just an emotional gimmick?'

We'd heard prophecies in churches before. But those always seemed to be on the general side. These words were rather specific! Jen and I looked at each other and began to slide down in our seats so that the lady wouldn't notice us. I remember making some joke to Jen about not letting her catch her eye or else she would also be invited up to the front for 'ministry'. Just then I looked up to see who would be the next victim. The woman was looking directly at me!

Jen and I had married in August 1987. We moved to Chesham Bois in Buckinghamshire, where I was offered a position as youth worker for an Anglican church in the heart of 'greenbelt' country. The area is sandwiched between two busy towns, Chesham and Amersham.

People often talk about it as 'leafy' because it was born out of a large wooded area.

It is the province of the privileged. There are large houses adorned with security lights and cameras, but also smaller, starter homes for young couples and families. Because of its excellent education system Buckinghamshire has been the carrot drawing many families from other areas to settle here – with its easy access to central London on the Tube. The wealth of the area is startlingly obvious to people when they first arrive.

We felt nervous about accepting a position in that locality. I had never lived in an area like it before. It made me feel small. I called out to God for help. I knew that this was one calling I would find hard, but if it really was where God was calling us, then all we needed to do was trust him. We felt so unprepared for the work – and were overwhelmed by the wealth as well as the needs we found in the local community.

For the first few months, with little in the way of furniture, we slept on the floor until we could save enough to buy our first bed. We didn't really encounter hardship in the true sense of the word. In fact, we didn't seem to mind not having furniture, and so on. We had enough to get by.

But the change from dating to actually living together took some working out. We both had our own ideas of where we wanted to go and how things should be done. There were tears, upsets and misunderstandings as we worked out how two independent people could and would live together – while seeking to work together as examples for young people. The secret to all of that was prayer. Even though we didn't always pray together at the same time, prayer was at the heart of our day. And of course, we tried our best to maintain a sense of humour!

Dealing with people's perceptions was one of our hardest challenges. Many in the church at that time expected us to be like the previous youth leader – who'd been a dynamic up-front speaker – but we didn't fit that description. Our boss and minister, Mike Hill, gave us the space and time to be ourselves. He let us make the youth work what we wanted – which was a living expression of God's love for each other and the world. Slowly we got to know the locals, the area and the young people. It was exciting to be able to serve God in that way. And we had an amazing, caring team around us. Two years after moving there, we came to the point in our lives where we were starting to see some fruit from our labours for God.

The church youth group was growing and the children's groups were growing. We felt more and more comfortable with our youth work, which proved to be a door for God to use in challenging us to move on. One of the things we had learned in our ministry was that, like it or not, the Church is not perfect.

There was one thing that really annoyed me, and that was gossip. I think it annoyed me the most because I was quite good at it. And in Christian circles the word 'gossip' was usually changed into the word 'sharing'. There was much 'sharing' going on in the church. We tried not to have much to do with it – when it was just gossip. Sometimes the sharing was directed at us personally; at other times it was directed at the leadership because we were changing too many things, or were going too slowly or too fast.

One of the first jobs we were asked to do was to disband a long-running youth movement from the church. That met with fierce opposition. The gossip that came out of that did untold damage to us as a couple – and to many others in the church.

We had threatening phone calls and hate letters. There were tough meetings with leaders who obviously didn't have the mind of Christ, as they spoke out viciously against us in certain circles. It took a couple of years for the gossip to die down, which then allowed God to bring healing and growth to the youth ministry.

We began to ask God to direct us in our future together, and to show us very clearly what his perfect will was for our lives. We also asked him to show us whether he wanted us to have children or not. We so wanted to share our prayer requests with another Christian, but were scared of what people might say. After all, we were in a leadership role. We needed to keep up the image of being in control of all areas of our lives. We were also afraid of being looked at and pitied as the ones who couldn't have children, which we didn't think would be too helpful. So we kept it to ourselves and to God.

For three years, Jen and I had been trying to have children. It wasn't that we had some medical problem. We were privileged enough to have a doctor who's a Christian. His name is Bryn Neal and he has his surgery in Amersham. He's a very wise and godly man – and he always brought the spiritual side of things into the equation because he knew we were Christians. He said it was in God's hands and just to trust and wait. We couldn't seem to produce even a glimmer of hope with the pregnancy test kits. So we trusted God and continued to pray for his will to be done in our lives.

'When are you going to have children?' people would say. 'Have you planned anything yet? What is the problem? Do you need help?' They were difficult years, to put it mildly.

Having children was an issue in our lives because it

was something that we'd wanted separately. When we married we thought of nothing else but one day having a child. When you dream of something so much, you then try to make it become a reality.

In our second and third years together, the desire grew. We sought to plan for a child practically. When you see families together you romanticise about how it would be to have children to love and care for.

After a couple of years of trying, nothing happened. And we knew that our feelings of loss would never be filled with other people's words of comfort. We had to trust that God had everything in his perfect plan. Inside there was hurt, emptiness and a fear that God might actually say 'no' to us. I wanted to show myself that I could be a good father. I knew I would make things different for my own family – if only God gave me that chance. If no children came, there was no way I could ever prove that to myself.

That kind of thinking can become destructive. You end up looking at other people with children – and feeling angry that they have what you don't. At times you greet the news of a friend's pregnancy with sadness rather than joy. When I realised we were starting to react like that, I knew it was becoming obsessive. We wanted to take that feeling to God and seek his will in our lives radically.

At the same time we became more involved with working among families – trying to give dry advice to those who had more experience of child-rearing than we did! We felt isolated and lonely. It was always difficult to look at the young children with whom we worked and think that we had none of our own. But God was about to answer our prayers. It was all in his perfect timing – even though we couldn't see it then.

For a number of years we had attended an event in the

north of England called the Evangelists' Conference, organised by the Evangelical Alliance. We were looking forward to that time with anticipation. We had been feeling spiritually dry and wanting to renew our vision and seek God's guidance for our future. Little did we know that the conference was to change the course of our lives.

After an introductory meal, the conference sessions started. Just to meet with a few hundred people who shared a common vision and love for Jesus was enough. But we also found the worship and teaching extremely beneficial.

The second day, after breakfast, Jen and I had arrived early at the main conference room, finding it empty apart from a few people practising music, and took our seats. No sooner had we sat down than an old friend, Stuart Pascall, walked into the hall. Stuart had been my third-year tutor at Bible college when I was studying evangelism. At Moorlands, Stuart had seemed to be the only person who believed in me – the only one to believe that God could use someone like me to achieve his will and further his kingdom in the world.

Stuart was also one of the people who'd interviewed me for the place at college. An itinerant evangelist, he would often be travelling around the UK, preaching and teaching. He had joined the staff at Moorlands as the Director of Evangelism and was also responsible for teaching doctrine – which he did in a very systematic and entertaining way. His informative style appealed to me. But it was his spirituality that drew me to him. Here was a man who prayed and trusted God to answer prayer.

As soon as I saw Stuart at the conference, I knew we had to ask for his prayers. Here was someone we could trust. And he was known to be a man of prayer.

'Jenni,' I said to my wife, 'why don't we ask Stuart to

pray for us?' We looked at each other and agreed to tell Stuart about our childlessness.

As we approached Stuart, he greeted us and we asked if he could pray for us about something. Stuart agreed and invited us to join him in one of the smaller rooms to the side of the main meeting hall. I was anxious not to take too much of his time, as the meeting was soon to begin. As I sat down, with Jenni next to me, I looked across the small room at Stuart, who smiled and asked how he could pray for us.

It seemed like forever before I replied. I explained that for a few years Jen and I had being trying to have children – but hadn't really got anywhere. Stuart listened and then said he would love to pray for us. He began to pray, asking God to speak and reveal his will for our lives. I thought he was in the middle of his prayer when he asked us to look at him.

'As I was praying for you,' Stuart explained, 'I felt God speak to me and know I have something to say to you. God has heard your prayers and does indeed want you to have children.'

Before that moment our heads had been bowed in prayer. But we looked up when he spoke. Holding each other's hand, we were rather awestruck by his words. It took a few moments for them to sink in. Direct prophecy like that was something we'd heard others talk about – but had never before experienced for ourselves. I suppose we were a little sceptical inside. But as soon as Stuart uttered those words, something within us jumped! It was like an inner confirmation that this was of God.

Stuart added, 'I felt that God wants you to have children and that he will begin this work in either December or maybe January. I don't know why December or January is significant. But please pray and ask God to confirm it, if that is his will for you.'

Never before had anyone ever spoken to me in that way. Never before had I felt such a strong sense of the presence of God as I did in that small room. We prayed for a couple of minutes together before returning to the main meeting hall. I had wanted to ask Stuart for prayer about the second matter that was on our hearts – our future. But time was against us for now. As we returned to the conference hall, we noticed that the meeting had begun. We took the only available seats, at the front.

Stuart's words haunted me. I couldn't get them out of my mind as we sang some praise songs. After what seemed only a couple of minutes, Noel Richards, who was leading the worship, invited everyone to form small groups where we were, so that we could pray. I can't remember what we were asked to pray for, as I was still thinking about what Stuart had said. As I looked around the room at the many groups of people praying, someone caught my attention. An elderly lady, who had been sitting at the back of the room, was walking around the various praying groups obviously looking for something.

'Why isn't she praying?' I asked myself. 'And where is she going? Perhaps the prayer session is too much for her.'

I wasn't aware that she was making her way to our seats. Nor was I aware of the fact that while I was judging her for not praying, I wasn't in a state of prayer either – choosing rather to focus my attention on her rather than on Jesus. I returned to the group and buried my head in my hands, in what Adrian Plass calls the 'shampoo position'. Then in the middle of the prayer session I felt a hand on my shoulder. As I looked up I recognised the lady who'd been walking around.

'Excuse me,' she said, addressing our little prayer group, 'I feel I need to pray for this couple.' I noticed that her other hand was gently resting on Jen's shoulder. 'Would you mind if I prayed for you?' she asked me and Jen.

'Not at all,' I answered, completely anxious as we knew nothing about this lady. I wondered how she knew we were a couple. Up to this day we have never met her again. We don't know anything about her – only that God used her to speak to us. Without even asking our names or anything about us, this woman started to pray.

'I think I would like to share something with you,' said the lady, midway through her prayer. Without waiting for us to ask her what she wished to share with us, she continued, 'As I was sitting at the back, I felt God wanted me to pray for you both. That's why I came over here. But I didn't know exactly how I should pray. Please feel free to accept this or reject it if you feel it is not from God. As I was praying, God spoke to me and asked me to say that he has heard your prayers, and that he wants you to have children. I don't know why, but I feel that December or January will be significant in the beginning of that process.'

We looked at each other in astonishment. Did she really say that? Before we could discuss it, she asked if she could pray for us some more. We agreed and so prayed again together.

'Are you praying about your future at the moment?' she asked. Sure enough, we had been seeking God's will about our future for some time. How was it that this lady, who we'd never met before, knew so much about us? It was one of those moments when time seemed to stand still. She spoke to us again.

'God has a great plan for your lives. God is preparing

you to serve him in a new way. He wants to take you from the orthodox to the unexpected, from the near to the far. God wants to prepare you to work with children. You will be a father to the fatherless and a mother to the motherless.'

For some time now God had been using us more and more with children. That was an area of ministry that we knew God was calling us into. But her following remarks didn't seem to fit in with what we thought was God's plan for our lives.

'God wants you to work with children,' the mystery woman continued, 'children who are homeless, hungry, abusing drugs and in need of his love.' She looked at us and asked us to pray about this. She added that we needed to pray about two words that she felt were very significant. The words were 'open doors'.

'It is as though there will be many doors facing you in the coming months,' she added. 'Those doors will be different opportunities for you. Please, and I can't stress this too strongly, pray that God will open the doors he wants you to walk through in service for him.'

She invited the small group we were sitting with, who also knew nothing about us, to pray for us – and then she left. I have never met her since, but know that God used her to speak to us and reveal to us his perfect will. Later in the security and silence of our own room, we analysed what had taken place that day. Our minds went over and over everything we remembered.

Jen, the clever one of the team, decided to write it all down so that we didn't forget what had been said to us. The thing we couldn't work out was the part about working with this particular group of children. Surely God wasn't thinking of sending us overseas? He must have some work for us in the UK.

On returning home after the conference, we decided to pray about what was prophesied over us, rather than 'share' it for prayer at church. We knew God would continue to lead us and open the doors for us if we remained faithful and spent time listening to him.

We'd never had any personal experiences of working specifically with homeless children. So that part of the prophecy was a total mystery to us. I had spent some time working in Toxteth in Liverpool, and then in St Paul's in Bristol, where I worked on the streets with homeless people. While I was in Bristol as part of my Bible college placement, I had also worked on a poor housing estate called Hartcliffe. There, I met children from needy families.

Some would spend their whole evening on the streets, hanging around on street corners, outside the youth club I was attached to or at any visible location. One little girl told me she was being abused. It broke my heart and made me withdraw inside myself for a few days while I thought of her life and her options for the future. I wondered if the prophecy that was given to us at the conference meant we were being called to that kind of youth work.

My background was subconsciously coming into this, as I felt the need to protect vulnerable children. After all, no one had really done it for me.

We had wanted to return to Jen's homeland, Australia, ever since we were married. We'd been there for our honeymoon. We saved up all our money and, together with gifts from friends, had enough for two flights to visit the glorious land down under in December 1990. Jen's parents had a house in Brisbane. That's in the heart of the sunshine state of Queensland. But they also had a house situated an hour's drive north on the coast near their parents' house. Most weekends they would stay there.

It was a lovely spot as the house was just ten minutes' walk from the long golden beaches, which were largely unspoilt. We would wander up and down the beach every day, walking the shore's edge and just talking about life and how wonderful God's creation is. I enjoyed the warm sunny days and occasional evening storms. The sky would light up for an hour or so as a tropical storm passed overhead.

It was great to be with Jen's family again. We really enjoyed our time with them. But we were having a hard time because Jen kept feeling ill. We blamed the food on the plane. But after much thought and medicine, we decided to check just one more time to see if she was pregnant. I will never forget that moment when Jen called to me from upstairs and asked me to join her. With a big smile on her face, she told me that the test indicator had turned blue. After all that waiting and praying, it was confirmed: Jen was pregnant.

Our joy at having the test confirmed was so great. It seemed there was nothing else to think of apart from babies. We were, and still are, so grateful to God for his faithfulness. Certainly what Stuart and the elderly lady had said about December or January being important was right.

It was such a significant month for us when Jen conceived. A new door was opening for us. In our joy and excitement about Jen's pregnancy, we continued to pray to God about our future. We focused especially on the two words that were given to us at the conference – 'open doors'. Those two words were at the forefront of our prayers each day.

As the weekend approached, I asked Jen where she thought we should go to church that Sunday. We were eager to meet with other Christians and give praise to

God for answering our prayers. Jen suggested we look for a church near to her parents' house. Then we wouldn't have far to travel on Sunday morning. There didn't seem to be any churches close by. But as we drove along a road not too far from where we were staying, we noticed a sign above a warehouse that said, 'Jesus is Lord!'

We turned off the main road and drove into the warehouse complex. The sign was situated above a large grey warehouse that looked uninviting from the outside. A notice was hanging up in the window. It invited all to join in worship at the church each Sunday at 10.00 a.m. Sunday morning came and we set off for church, a little anxious about this new place we were going to visit. On arrival we were handed a notice sheet and took a seat towards the back as the service started. I remember it being very hot and wondered if it was to be a long service. How would I cope?

The building was also grey inside. But it was decorated with brightly coloured banners and signs that proclaimed Jesus as Lord of all the earth. About 150 people were present, including children and young people. The service was well organised and an excellent band of musicians led us in a great time of lively worship. After a few songs of praise and the usual church notices -- which seem to be the same in any country around the globe – the speaker was introduced.

A slim, well-dressed lady stood up and began to read from the Bible. I slouched back in my chair as I listened. Then in astonishment I watched her invite certain people up to the stage for prayer or because, as she said, she had a word from God for them. It was at that point that she claimed to have a word for me.

'Sir,' she said, 'can you please come up here?' No one ever called me sir – that was the first thing that threw me!

I looked around to make sure it was really me she was talking to. Then an overwhelming sense of fear entered my whole body. It wasn't as if I was a member at that church. I had never been there before. And she knew nothing about me. What a way to treat people on their first visit to church!

I was reluctant to move. I was hoping she would move on to someone else. But she persisted, and invited me again to come forward. It was a long and painful walk from our comfortable back-row seat to the front. I'd only got halfway up the aisle when she asked me if the woman next to me was my wife. I stopped and looked at Jen just to make sure. Then I nodded.

'Can she come up also?' the lady asked.

'I'm sure she would love to,' I thought inside, as Jen walked up the aisle and joined me in my long and lonely walk to the stage. I was asking myself why we couldn't have chosen another type of church. The woman spoke to the congregation, saying that it was a real privilege to have us both in the church that morning and that they had been called upon by God to pray for us.

I felt my legs shaking inside my trousers. I was wondering what it must have looked like from the front row.

'You're visiting here, aren't you?' asked the lady speaker.

'Yes,' I replied. No use hiding now, I thought.

Then she said something that struck me dumb. The lady turned to me and said without hesitation, 'Now, you're praying about open doors, aren't you?' I nodded and looked at Jen, wondering how on earth she knew that. She continued, saying that she felt God was preparing us for a new ministry.

'This new ministry,' she told us, 'will be with children

– children who are homeless and take drugs.' She felt that God had called us to that church today so they could pray for us. It was hard to describe our feelings. Inside I wondered how she knew all this stuff about us. The blood was rushing through our veins. We were very nervous and totally excited – all at the same time!

We felt the hands of the bodyguards on our backs as she began to pray for us. It was all over in two minutes – no fuss, no falling, no dramatic stuff, just a gentle word of assurance from God that he was with us, preparing us for something new. We returned to our seats very different and totally assured that God was in control of whatever he was calling us to. All we needed to do was to trust and wait. It was important for us to know the doors that God was opening, and when he did, we would have to trust him enough to walk through them.

'Did this really happen?' I asked myself. My mind couldn't even concentrate on the rest of the service. Eager to find out more, we rushed over to the lady after the meeting. I wanted to ask her about it – just to prove that it had really happened. When she confirmed over again what she had said to us, and nothing more, we tightly held each other's hands, squeezing more with every confirmation. It really was true. That made us both feel special and humble. Then we did what Mary did – who 'pondered these things in her heart'.

4

They Shoot Children, Don't They?

Early morning in Guatemala City. The sun was just breaking through the heat haze and car fumes. A BBC TV crew were shadowing *los bomberos*, the local volunteer fire and rescue service. They'd been called out to the side of a bridge – where the body of a young boy had been found. The lad had been murdered, and then unceremoniously dumped in the long grass. The *bomberos* carried his stiff little body and placed it in the back of their pick-up truck.

The crew also filmed a charity worker talking with a local girl. She described one afternoon when she and three of her friends were kidnapped by police officers from outside a market stall. According to this report, the kids were taken to the cemetery, where they were tortured. The girl said she managed to get away. Her friends, however, weren't so lucky. They were allegedly found dead some time later.

Their bodies were covered with horrific wounds. Their eyes had been burned out. Their tongues had been cut. And their ears were hacked off. It was a sign, a warning. And the message was: don't say anything, don't hear anything and don't see anything. But this wasn't the work of some cult or weird fanatical group. Those kinds of horrors were happening all the time. And they weren't just confined to Guatemala.

After returning to England from Australia, Jen and I had felt a real sense of God's presence and power upon us. We were eager to seek God for his perfect will for our lives. And we continued to pray about the words we'd been given in England and in Australia – 'open doors'. It was in the February of that year, 1991, that we sat down one evening after church to watch television.

It had been a busy day of youth meetings in the morning, extra preparation in the afternoon, church in the evening, followed by youth group. Part of our way of relaxing has usually been to make a cup of tea and sit together in front of the TV. Our viewing was usually restricted to the news, some films and documentaries.

The *Everyman* series was often thought-provoking, and sometimes a great resource programme for material for the youth group discussions. So we tuned in. A documentary came on, called *They Shoot Children, Don't They?*, which highlighted the plight of the street children of Guatemala. We watched as the programme explained how so many little children had been abandoned to the streets by parents who didn't want them any more. Others were runaways from homes where they'd been abused. They all had a different story to tell. But all had one thing in common. No one cared for them.

The faces of those children etched themselves on to our minds as we saw them begging on the streets, stealing and getting high on shoe glue. They had no other way out. It all seemed so hopeless. At least something was being done to help the children by the workers featured in the programme. Yet it was still a drop in the ocean.

The BBC film crew were taken to various parts of Guatemala City. They gave the viewer a glimpse into the life of a street child. Then the sequences were shown that featured the young boy's body and the girl's report of horrific deaths and mutilations. The reports made me feel sick. The programme finished. I sat there, horrified at all that I had just seen.

'How can anyone do this to children?' I asked Jen.

She, too, had felt very saddened by the harrowing account of little children having to live on the streets of Latin America. And what made it worse was that the police were allegedly responsible for killing and torturing those youngsters. The very people we'd expect to protect the children from violence turned out to be the ones carrying out the wishes of business people and others who saw the children as just common thieves – and a potential threat to their livelihood.

The following morning those scenes depicted on the television were still fresh in my mind. I knew I needed to do something to help. So I wrote off to an organisation working in Guatemala, requesting information. At the same time I bought a book about street children. I started to wonder what it would be like to be eight years old and living on the streets of a major city. That thought stayed with me as Jen and I began to grow increasingly interested and concerned about the plight of the street children of Latin America.

Shortly after, an information pack arrived. Jen and I were organising the young people in our church to raise some money for the street children. I explained to the youth group something of the suffering of these children and how we could practically help them.

As the months went by, we continued to seek God and his will for our lives – and what doors he was going to open up for us. It was as if, from the February of 1991 to the September, we were being prepared without knowing it. We were praying about this new ministry God had for us. And at the same time we were becoming more and more involved in the subject of street children in Latin America. It became a passion for me. It was something that I thought a lot about each day.

However, I knew God would never call us to leave our comfortable home in Chesham Bois to go and live overseas. God knew that the ministry there was going well. Furthermore, we were making all sorts of plans for the arrival of our first child. I had decorated the house – and we were very happy with all we had. 'Surely God wouldn't ask us to give all this up?' we thought to ourselves.

On the morning of August 29th 1991 a very special girl was born. Weighing in at 7lb 12½oz, Katelyn Dyason made her entry into the world. It was a very emotional experience for us to be trusted with the responsibility and joy of parenthood. Life was never going to be the same, as we began to settle into our new roles of being Mum and Dad to this long-awaited little girl.

Whatever calling God had upon our lives, we knew it would now be as a family. We thought that his plan for our lives would be to settle down and enjoy all the blessings he was pouring out upon our lives. It was good to sit down and plan school assemblies, youth group meetings and home improvements. Generally we had become more settled with life.

What a mistake that was!

There had been another busy day of church meetings. And we were looking forward to sitting down in front of the television that evening. The documentary about the street children in Guatemala – the one we had seen seven months before – was going to be repeated. We were organised this time and were going to video it so that we could show it to the youth group.

The documentary was just as distressing as I had remembered – especially the scene where a little boy is found dead on the streets and some aid workers carry his little body, now stiff with rigor mortis, into a van for burial. His life didn't seem to matter to anyone.

At the end of the programme Jen and I just looked at each other. We admitted that God had spoken to our hearts through the programme. We knew he was calling us to go to Guatemala and help the street children. It wasn't, as some have thought, an idea of mine that Jen joined in with. We both felt the calling of God upon our lives that evening. We talked and prayed together. And we thought back over all that had taken place since the time we prayed with Stuart Pascall nine months before.

There were no signs that night of what the next step would be in God's plan for our lives. But there was just a deep conviction in our hearts that this was generally what God wanted for us. After we prayed together, Jen went upstairs and, at her bedside, found a little book in which she'd written down the things we felt God was going to do in our lives. She brought the book down. We hadn't read over the notes she had made. In fact, that was the first time I had seen them at all. Yet the more we read the notes, the more we remembered the 'open doors' part of the story.

It all seemed to fit in with what we were now thinking. God was indeed calling us to be a father to the fatherless and a mother to the motherless. Everything that was prophesied about us was coming true. Guatemala was certainly an unexpected place: the prophecy said we would go from the orthodox to the unexpected. It was certainly far from home: the prophecy had said the new ministry would take us far from home. It was all about working with children who were homeless and were taking drugs

– which again was exactly what the prophecy had said.

'But is this the place where doors are going to open?' we asked ourselves. We were buzzing with excitement – and with fear of the unknown. It was hard to sleep that night as my mind was filled with wonder, excitement and joy.

The next morning I woke early and started to pray. I began my prayer time by thanking God that he should look upon even us and want to use us. My thoughts and prayers then turned to Latin America and the street children as I explained to God all that had happened. As if he didn't know!

I asked God for one thing. If he was calling us to go overseas and minister his love to street children, then we would need someone in the UK who could act as a link-person for us. That would be someone who would organise our finances, distribute news and prayer letters and handle any correspondence that came to us. That person would need to be a very special comrade, and would need to be directly called by God, as they would play a significant role in our lives.

At breakfast I explained to Jen that I had asked God to give us someone who would be a link-person for us. If he did, we would know that it was God's will that we go to Latin America and work with the street children!

Jen was still in shock from the previous night. She didn't really take on board what I had just said. We chatted frantically over breakfast about what all this was going to mean for us as a family and our ministry at St Leonard's.

Just after breakfast we had a phone call from a man we had previously met in church one Sunday evening. His name was Ian Edwards. He wanted to know if Jen, Katelyn and I would like to go for lunch the following day. We accepted his kind offer, wondering why he wanted us to join him and his wife for a meal. I expected that he just wanted to talk to us about his teenage daughters and their involvement in the church youth group.

When we arrived at the Edwards' household, Ian introduced us to his wife, also Jenni, who we knew as little about as we did Ian. We chatted for a while about the church and how we had met.

Then after lunch, Ian pulled me to one side and said he felt he needed to say something to me. My initial thought was that I was in trouble! But he said that he had been praying for us. He had thought that if ever God called us to go and work overseas with children and we needed a link-person in England, he felt he should be the one!

I remember feeling the hairs on the back of my neck stand on end as Ian said that. It was a real joy to share with Ian all that had taken place to date and how, only yesterday morning, I had asked God to give us such a person. Ian rushed upstairs and brought down a little notebook.

In it he kept notes about the sort of things God had said to him. He showed me that for about a year he had been praying about this – and now felt the time was right to approach me. After further discussion I found out that he, too, had seen the BBC documentary, and was particularly moved by it. Now we knew God was indeed opening the doors for us.

After being with Ian and his wife, once again we were feeling very special that Almighty God should want to use us – and especially to speak directly to us in this manner. It was truly wonderful.

Jen went home and I went to have my weekly meeting with the rector – my boss, Mike Hill. Mike was a wise man and always listened to what I had to say. That day I was feeling very fearful of explaining to Mike about the way we felt God was leading us. If I told him that we were thinking of leaving the parish, then maybe he would be upset. But I knew he had to be told.

Mike's house was just across the road from Ian Edwards' home, a short walk away. En route, I tried to put the events of the previous six months in some sort of order so that I could effectively explain all we knew God had said. The fact that this new ministry meant that we would have to leave the parish was just beginning to come home to me as I walked up Mike's drive. I paused just before I rang the doorbell and prayed to God for strength.

When I did ring, Mike answered almost immediately. He invited me into the kitchen, where we made a cup of tea, and then we walked into his study. He sat down in his chair and looked into my eyes in the way that pastors and vicars do.

'So, what's happening?' he asked me.

I was very nervous. However, I gritted my teeth and explained to Mike all that had happened. I went through the whole story from beginning to end. I made sure that I wasn't glossing over the implications for us all.

'Praise God!' was Mike's unexpected response, as he sat back in his chair. It certainly wasn't the reaction I thought I was going to have to face! He went on to tell me that he had woken up in the middle of the night a few months previously, and knew he had to pray for us. Mike said that he had felt God say we were going to leave the parish the following summer and set up a new work for him. He knew that something like this would happen, and told me how he had been praying for us to leave next summer.

'Don't get me wrong,' Mike explained, 'it's not that I want you to leave. It's just that I know God is calling you into something new.'

Looking back, it all seemed like a dream world. Things were happening so fast that I had no time to step aside and think it all through. I had to accept that if this was God leading us, then all we needed to do was to follow. Mike then said he was to have a missionary committee meeting that night. It would be good if he could share all this with them – and ask them to consider supporting an exploratory trip to Guatemala.

I could see that the whole vision had already taken root in his heart. And as we talked together, we both got more and more excited.

'If you can contact a travel agent,' Mike went on to say, 'and phone me back with the price of a flight out to Guatemala, I will see if we can support you in some way.'

We prayed together. Then I started to walk home with all this spinning around in my head. But a troublesome thought occurred to me. Where was Guatemala? I knew it was in Latin America somewhere, but hadn't a clue of its exact location. I had in my mind that it was somewhere near Brazil.

It was on my way back home that I remembered how, the year before, I had a very clear picture placed in my mind. The picture was of a children's toy box with toys crammed inside and a teddy bear sitting on one corner. There were blocks in front of the toy box which spelt out the word TOYBOX.

The name The Toybox Charity had come into my mind. And I remember that I told Jenni about it. But she had felt that it hadn't meant anything to her. It was a very clear picture to me, and I still have it in my mind today. I can even remember the exact location where God revealed it to me: it was at the corner of the road to my house.

It was the corner of our road that had brought the vision sharply back into my mind now. I was not aware of the traffic passing by or what the weather was like. I just had a real sense of the presence of God. From there, I ran on towards our house, only half a minute away.

After pausing briefly at that spot, I headed for the front door. Jen opened the door with excitement in her voice, saying we'd had a phone call. She explained that while I had been meeting with Mike, she had received a phone call from a Christian travel company in Bristol called Worldwide Christian Travel. They had rung to say that they had cheap flights to Latin America – would we be interested? I was bowled over. So was Jen. Apparently the travel company had found our names from a UK directory of Christian workers, and were phoning around with the latest offers. At that particular time they had discount flights to Latin America.

If we hadn't realised already, we knew then – God was clearly speaking to us. I phoned the company back and asked for prices to Guatemala. Later that same week, I phoned them again and booked two flights to Guatemala – one for myself and the other for Ian Edwards. The week after all that happened, we received a letter from an organisation called SAMS with details of their summer Spanish language training courses.

The letter was not directed at us specifically. But it was informing us, its supporters, of a summer course that might be of interest. Since the language in Guatemala was Spanish, it was obvious that we needed to study – and that seemed to be yet another thing that God used to assure us he was in control.

And when it came to studying another language, I knew God needed to be watching over us and planning our next move. For I had never been any good at the English language – let alone Spanish! I prayed and asked God to give me the gift of Spanish rather than having to learn it.

Surely he could do that, couldn't he, I thought. But God chose for me to learn the hard way – just like everyone else!

The church in Tunbridge Wells where Jen and I had met wrote to us after hearing about where we felt God was calling us. They offered to support us as missionaries. Apparently they had been supporting someone through SAMS. But the missionary had come home and was no longer going to serve God overseas. So the church had been thinking about who to support next.

It was at that stage that I wrote to the church, explaining the call we had from God to go to Guatemala. And that confirmed to them who they could now support as missionaries. We could see God not only in the big decisions, but also in the little ones.

Then a letter came which confirmed yet again that all this was God's will for us. We had been praying about the words 'open doors'. We knew by then that Latin America was where God was calling us. Shortly after I booked the flights to Guatemala for myself and Ian, a letter arrived from one of the lecturers at Moorlands.

It was just a general prayer letter. It was obvious that the sender knew nothing of what God was doing in our lives at that point. However, he had written at the bottom of his prayer letter the words: 'Latin America is where the doors are open.' It was just another part of a very exciting time when God really confirmed to us over and over again that he was in supreme control. All we had to do was to trust him.

5

The Streets of Guatemala

Their clothes were dirty and well worn. Most had no shoes – some had poor examples of them. Their faces gave nothing away. Their eyes were empty and dark. They stood around inhaling glue from a small plastic bag. The experience seemed to take them away to another place.

They were the street children. And we were finally meeting them, face to face.

Despite their appearance, they seemed happy inside. It was good to chat, through an interpreter, with these youngsters – and with the staff from a city refuge. Most of the children we talked with expressed their desire to leave the streets. They wanted to go to school or get a job, raise a family, and live like everyone else. They were just normal children.

Seeing street children in the flesh for the very first time was incredible. No longer were they children on a leaflet or images on a TV screen. These kids were real. Their hair was unkempt. Some of them looked as if they'd tried to cut their own hair, with messy results. It was also matted with dirt. That made their hair look thick and dark. Most children wore very few clothes. Those they did wear were ragged and torn.

As I shook one boy's hand, I noticed the tattoos and scars on his arms – and the long black nails on his hands. He wasn't wearing any shoes. But his feet had toughened to the streets. A very hard skin had formed on his soles. It may have been unattractive, but it enabled him to walk over the roughest of surfaces – even glass – without injuring his feet. The children's eyes didn't focus on one thing for very long as they inhaled deeply from their glue bags. At times their eyes would roll up into their heads before focusing again on the deflated bag in their hands.

I didn't appreciate then how much they had really suffered. Our interpreter told us stories that began to make us feel angry – accounts of abuse and abandonment, rape and torture. It all seemed so hopeless. What future did these children really have, we wondered.

It was March 1992 when Ian Edwards and I left our comfortable homes in Chesham Bois, Buckinghamshire, and flew to Guatemala. On the way, we thought back together over the BBC programme and retold the stories that had challenged us. That fuelled our imaginations as to what was waiting for us in Guatemala. We tried out a few Spanish phrases on each other – and assured ourselves that we would manage to buy two beers and a loaf of bread!

We decided to watch the in-flight movie to help pass the next nine hours until we reached Miami Airport to change for Guatemala. After the film, I read through a Guatemalan guide book. I was trying to remember as much of the history of the country as I could. If Jen and I were going to live there, it was important for us to appreciate the culture – and to understand that we would need to know something of Guatemala's past.

Its glorious history seemed to have been in stark contrast to the poverty-ridden streets of today. Apparently, most archaeologists agree that this ancient kingdom was the cultural centre of the New World. The much-documented Mayan civilisation, the jewel of that society, was said to have originated there. The Maya developed a unique society that boasted a complex social, political and scientific structure.

Mayan research into the fields of mathematics, astronomy and the measurement of time is truly astonishing. This region was to the New World as Athens was to the old. This is where everything happened. Even today, Guatemala is described as 'the country of eternal spring' – and the tourist brochures welcome 'adventure-lovers' to its jungles, plains, mountains and lakes.

Yet both Ian and I had fears and apprehensions regarding the Guatemala of the late twentieth century. How would we cope seeing the street children? How would they react to us? How would we communicate with them in our basic phrase-book Spanish? Would we return alive?

Ironically, because of altitude, the capital, Guatemala City, is free of most tropical diseases. But there are other dangers. And we were to discover them for ourselves. On arrival there we felt a rare mixture of fear and excitement as the noise and smells of this exotic country greeted us. It's quite different from the country's ancient beginnings and Spanish colonial heritage.

Modern and cosmopolitan, every day the city welcomes hundreds of travellers from the United States, Europe and Latin America. The first sights you meet in this cosmopolitan metropolis are the gleaming, modern buildings sparkling in the sun. I remember looking around and seeing men with machine guns. Then we were met by a group of local people competing and clamouring to change money, carry our luggage – which hadn't arrived yet – or show us to a taxi. It was all rather overwhelming.

As we struggled through the crowd and emerged from Guatemalan customs, to our relief we were met by a woman holding up our names on a notice board. She was from the agency we had first contacted after watching the TV documentary. She took us to our hotel and promised to return the following day to show us their project with the street children.

It was scary. We'd been left alone in a large city to fend for ourselves. Everything we'd read about Guatemala – its police force, political killings, kidnappings, death squads, the civil war and of course the street children – had all come to mind that night as we tried to sleep. I'd woken only occasionally to see a cockroach running up the wall or to hide under the covers as I was swarmed over by mosquitoes.

The next day I woke early to the sound of diesel engines. The city was awake – and from the sounds of them, the buses were in serious need of repair. Ian and I dressed and took our seats for breakfast, trying to cope with ordering cereal and a cup of coffee. We then left the relative security of our hotel and stood in anticipation on the front doorstep to be collected by our guide. Buses rushed by, leaving a blanket of thick black smoke behind, as they did their best to pick up customers from every conceivable collection point.

A small minibus pulled up. It was the agency that had met us the previous night. We were taken on a tour of their children's homes and the city refuge for street children. I felt way out of my depth when a large group of street boys approached us and asked us our names. We were stuck for words, but Ian did his best at trying to explain that we were not from Guatemala. I think that fact was obvious to the youths!

The refuge was situated on a busy street right in the heart of downtown zone one. Even the imposing high iron gates at the entrance had become a kind of 'home' to a small group of street children. They stared at us as we entered. After going through the gates, we walked into a very bright patio area decorated with a few pot plants and flowers.

A couple of children were mopping the floor with two very dirty cloths wrapped around a pole. Around the courtyard were various rooms – the clinic, counselling room, kitchen, laundry, store-room, showers and bed-rooms. The bedrooms were just large rooms with a pile of foam mattresses in one corner. It was all very basic. But the children were glad that it was a step off the streets for them.

The director of the refuge showed us round and introduced us to the staff and children. We asked him about the violence in Guatemala. He told us that he had received phone calls telling him not to work with the street children any more. If he did, the callers had warned, he would be killed. Apparently it was not uncommon for those who work with the children to be treated the same way as the kids themselves. Staff laid their lives on the line by working with the street children.

After looking around the refuge and meeting some of the kids who'd left the life of the streets to take shelter, we decided just to stay a while and try and watch how they worked with the children.

Walking back to our hotel that afternoon, we witnessed one of the street children we had met earlier, eight-year-old Hugo, trying to rob a passer-by of his wallet. The man decided to fight. The small boy produced a knife and began to threaten the man with it. We felt that we had to help and tried to communicate to the boy that this was not good. I expect he thought we were just crazy people, but he remembered seeing us in the refuge and just shouted at us and walked off. The man ran in the opposite direction, glad of a little gringo intervention.

Stealing to survive is a deadly game. While we were in Guatemala a child was shot dead by police for stealing a motorist's sunglasses. Two other street children were caught breaking into a car to steal the radio, which they would have sold to the market traders the following day. The children were beaten by police.

It was a challenging time for us over the next few days as we witnessed a reality that we'd rather not have known. We walked for about four hours one evening with the street team, getting to know the city after dusk. It was a hot evening and the streets were dusty and dry. Even though it was night, the streets were alive.

The darkness above contrasted with the street lights which illuminated Guatemala City and gave everything an orange glow. Now and again we came across a night-club or bar where groups of people stood around outside and talked. They looked at us suspiciously. Sometimes we were followed by little children, eager to find out what we were up to. After about four hours of walking, our initial fear had subsided. Now there was only a deep sadness. We were overwhelmed by the extremes we had witnessed between the very rich – with their grand houses surrounded by high walls and armed guards – and the very poor who lived in tin shacks with no electricity, sanitation or security. It seemed so unfair. I felt very angry with myself at the way I had lived and the things I had spent my money on, when other people had to live like this.

Daytime brought similar revelations. Just up the road from our hotel room was a small park. At first we didn't notice that there was a small group of street children sitting at one end of the park. We sat down and took out a loaf of bread and a packet of cheese we had just bought from a supermarket. As we made some sandwiches we looked around at the hustle of Guatemalan daily life.

Small groups of people were sitting around, chatting. Others were watching practical demonstrations of the latest 'should have' for your house. A child was wandering around with two large plastic bags of nuts, offering them at a bargain price. Then a young man came and sat down next to Ian and me and began to talk to us in English. He seemed very interested in us and what we were doing in Guatemala; then I clicked when he started asking us to go with him to a nearby hotel. He was obviously a male prostitute. This was probably not a good place for two men to be sitting eating their sandwiches!

The noise of the city was as constant as the heat. Because it was the hottest time of year, the ground was dry and dusty. The stench of bus fumes seemed to cling to our clothes everywhere we went. But despite those initial experiences, Guatemala had a charm about it that attracted us. We wanted to find out more.

My concern each day was that of safety – taking the usual precautions everywhere we went, taking care not to carry too much money and obvious expensive items, as well as constantly being aware of those around us. I wondered how my young family would cope in such a seemingly dangerous country. As I looked around I was anxious for our security – especially that of our six-month-old daughter. We were obviously not ready for the next big step. There would be much to do in preparation if we were going to move here. But we were going to do it together and knew that God would be with us through whatever was to come.

The two weeks that Ian and I spent in Guatemala changed both of our lives. The hardest part was getting on the plane, looking out of the little window and asking myself how I could communicate all this to Jen. As the plane took off I looked at the city below and cried. There was something of me that had remained behind. I felt a tug inside – something I knew was of God – calling me back, calling me to give myself for those below. Then I fell into a deep sleep.

On returning to England, life seemed very different. Those who've travelled around the world have been known to remark that England hardly changes. So much had happened to us in two weeks. Yet our families and friends were still exactly the same. We were keen to share what we had seen. I was eager to talk and pray with Jen.

She needed to know what I felt had been confirmed about our going to Guatemala. The director of the programme had invited us to move there in September and run one of the children's homes. He'd told me that if we felt this was something we would like to do, then we needed to raise £15,000 for the running costs of the home, our language training and other expenses.

Everything began to move very quickly as we prayed together about how we were going to respond to God's call upon our lives. Ian and another friend from our local church, David Stephenson, suggested that we set up a charity that could be used to handle donations. And so The Toybox Charity was born. Jen and I, with a small baby in tow, decided this was something God had led us to. And now it was our response to trust him, step out in faith and turn the vision into a reality.

With Mike Hill, we discussed our resignation – which would also mean giving up our home. We knew this was God's work and that he would provide for our needs. It was now up to us to take that step of faith and leave it in his hands. Our thoughts turned to how we would ever raise £15,000 in the next five months.

Other questions came to mind – what would happen to

us when we left the UK? What would our family and friends think? We faced a daunting future as there were so many unknown elements to it. And we weren't sure how things would work out – and exactly what we were being called to do in Guatemala.

Jen, Ian and I met together to discuss the future and pray for each other. We decided it would be right to invite two other people to join Ian in forming a board of trustees for Toybox and making it a registered charity. Ian's wife Jenni and fellow church member David Stephenson were invited and agreed to form the trustee board. Jenni would be an excellent help to Ian and was keen to help support us. David had always been there for us, and was a caring man who had a passion for everything in life. He was also an accountant and able to guide us wisely in our early steps.

After an initial meeting to agree how the trust was to be set up, we agreed on a mission statement for the charity: 'To promote awareness of the plight of the street children of Latin America and to support projects that seek to bring an end to their suffering.' David said he would look into the formation of the charity and would check to see if anyone was already using the name 'The Toybox Charity'. I was certain that no one was, as this was the name God had given me in a vision two years before. David did check, and found this was so. So we were able to register as 'The Toybox Charity'.

I was keen that the picture God had given me of the toy box should be made into a little logo that we could use on any literature we were going to produce. So I approached a talented young person in our church, Colin Pells, and he drew the picture that was still so clear in my mind. This is now our official logo for Toybox.

I then put down something on paper about what we felt

God was calling us to in Guatemala, and what specific things people could pray about. This was turned into a little leaflet which I photocopied and distributed to those who requested information about our forthcoming ministry. Some local churches and schools with whom I had contact asked Jen and me to go and share our calling with them. Some organised fund-raising events, and slowly money started to come in. After all that had happened, we had a strong faith that God was in total control and would provide for all our needs.

People around us were starting to feel challenged by the contrast between the absolute poverty and plight of the street children and the way they themselves were living. When you hear about those youngsters, it triggers an automatic response to look at your own life and how you can help. Others simply refused to let the pain of the kids reach their heart and replied with, 'Well, there is so much of it – and what about the homeless people in London?'

With regard to fund-raising, our local youth group organised the very first Tube Race, a sponsored race around the London Underground by teams of young people visiting as many stations as they could in one day. There were sales and special collections in churches. But most of the money came in from the most unexpected people – even from some of those who were initially opposed to us going to Guatemala.

Five months later, with very little help from us, God had provided £15,000. We were amazed to see the way he had touched people's hearts to give. Furthermore, a small group of friends had committed themselves to pray on a regular basis for us. That prayer meeting continued throughout our time in Guatemala and continues today, every Friday, at the Toybox office. Prayer was the powerhouse behind all that happened as we brought every need and concern to God.

Just before we left the UK, we sent our first newsletter, with a forwarding address and an explanation of the type of work we would be doing. That went to family and friends, which totalled about 150 people. The charity had begun with the idea of supporting us as a family. Some of our friends in the church were naturally concerned that we were going to such a violent country. Others questioned whether God would call a family to go to Guatemala – especially with a one-year-old baby.

Jen's family in Australia were even more anxious. They had found the whole idea of us going to work with street children in Guatemala really hard to deal with. It was important that we spent time with them before we set off for Guatemala. That trip was made possible by donations from several people. So we bought the plane tickets.

Just before we left for Australia, Jen was plagued with bad dreams. She said she had been troubled by doubts. They were going through her mind constantly. Then one night she awoke with the passage 2 Thessalonians 3:1–5 in her mind. After reading it, she was encouraged and never suffered the dreams again:

> Finally, brothers, pray for us that the message of the Lord may spread rapidly and be honoured, just as it was with you. And pray that we may be delivered from wicked and evil men, for not everyone has faith. But the Lord is faithful, and he will strengthen and protect you from the evil one. We have confidence in the Lord that you are doing and will continue to do the things we command. May the Lord direct your hearts into God's love and Christ's perseverance.

* * *

Our relatives down under were pleased to see us. When we stepped off the plane in Brisbane Jen's family were there to greet us. Their welcome was an encouraging sight. But it hid their true feelings of anxiety over our forthcoming trip to Guatemala.

In fact, they specifically asked us not to talk about it soon after we had cleared customs. They avoided any conversation about our new missionary calling. They didn't want to discuss the issue as they only wanted to spend time with us before we left – maybe for ever. It was a very hard thing to do. You could sense their fear and apprehension about this young family going into the unknown.

We had felt that this was a work God was calling us to for life. The street kids needed people around them who could stay with them and not see them as just another 'little project'. We had sold most of our furniture and all our electrical items, our car and anything of value. We weren't planning on returning to the UK for quite a few years – if ever! Jen's family realised that, and felt it would be best not to approach the subject.

One thing we did want to do while in Australia was to visit the church we had gone to the previous year. This was the place where a lady had received a word from God for us. The building was still there, and we felt a sense of anticipation as we went inside. Nothing much had changed.

We noticed that the church had a real burden for mission. Their banners proclaimed that Christ was to be preached throughout the nations and they showed us photos of the families they were currently supporting. There seemed an expectation that mission was part of your Christian walk – not just an option for people who were regarded as 'super-spiritual'.

The person who was preaching that day announced that he felt there were people in the congregation that God had been calling to serve him. His sermon was entitled 'Open doors'! He felt that there were some people in the congregation who were being called through open doors. He then went on to explain that God was opening up a door of opportunity to serve and preach the gospel, it was very challenging. I still have the notes from his sermon in my Bible. God spoke directly to us that day – and confirmed yet again his call upon our lives.

We asked about the woman who'd shared a word with us on our previous visit there. The church informed us that she had since left their congregation. But there was a way we could make contact with her. Literally just across the car park was a building where this woman worked. So we went over to see her.

At first she didn't recognise us. But as we explained who we were and what happened the day she prayed for us, she remembered the day – as well as some of the things she had said. It was wonderful to be able to sit with her and explain how God had used her and others to call us to Guatemala. It was obvious that our story encouraged her greatly, and she felt very humbled by the meeting. So did we.

We left Australia on a 'high', and with such a great expectation that God would do all sorts of amazing things through us. Yet we were just a young family, with a small but growing band of supporters. It was hard to think that this could be any major deal. This was just Dunc and Jen going to work with street children.

6

Hardly Home From Home

Guerrilla warfare; streets full of soldiers and tanks; the torture and murder of street children; a cholera epidemic; gangs of glue-sniffers; child prostitution; the attempted kidnapping of our own daughter – those were among the many horrors that we were about to face, on our arrival in Guatemala in September 1992.

We had come as a family. And we knew this time everything would be different. But just how different, we weren't sure. How can you prepare for such a shock to the system?

It was late evening and the airport terminal was heaving with people. We were concerned to get all our luggage and hoped that there was someone there to meet us. It was a hectic few minutes as luggage poured out on the one carousel from four different international flights.

Passengers fought for what they assumed were their bags. We kept hold of our three suitcases and a travel cot, even while greeting the person waiting for us. It was a smiling face that said 'hello' to these strangers from foreign shores. She was a representative from the agency with whom we had gone to work.

The driver with her helped carry our luggage to the car. We sat inside the small minibus and the driver locked the door.

'Keep the window closed,' he said. Then he got in the

minibus and drove off to the central part of town. On arrival at the hotel where we stayed that first night, all we wanted to do was sleep. We got Katelyn to sleep and looked out of the window over the city.

'Are we really here?' I thought to myself. Together we stood speechless, looking out at the neon lights in the streets, watching all the people going about their business.

After a sleepless night in the capital, we were taken to a place called Antigua where we were to begin our language training. 'We have found you a good family,' said the lady at the language school. She gave us directions to the house that was to become our home for the next three months. An important part of language training was to live with a Guatemalan family who spoke no English.

After a short journey we arrived at the house. Anxiously, we rang the doorbell. We were greeted by a lovely Guatemalan family who showed us to our room and ran through the rules and regulations of the house. Our hearts sank as we saw how small the room was. There was just enough space for two beds and a small cot. But it was clean and safe, and we were grateful to God for calling us to Guatemala. To make space for Katelyn to play, we pushed our beds together which gave her a little more room than she would have had on the floor.

The main difference between this house, which we were to know as home for these months, and ours in the UK was its openness. There were rooms centred around an internal courtyard that was open to the rain and sun. During the day the sun would shine and transform the courtyard into a gardener's paradise. In the evening it would be filled with mosquitoes.

The shower was at the end of the courtyard. It was basic but clean. We were reminded that toilet paper was not to be flushed down the toilet, but placed in a waste bin at the side! Inevitably, the container was always full – and teeming with cockroaches.

The house was situated on a main bus route, so we were woken each morning at 5.00 a.m. by buses revving up outside in the hope of attracting customers. Soon after the early buses had gone past the house it was time for the 5.30 a.m. firecrackers. Those were let off when it was someone's birthday.

A little further up the road was La Cruz, a popular tourist spot in Antigua. After a five-minute walk up the steep hill, you would arrive at a spectacular viewing-point of Antigua, marked with a large cross. Tourists were often held up at gunpoint there, and robbed of their precious holiday money. So it was a no-go area.

Our basic understanding of the Spanish language grew each day. We took turns in studying. I studied in the mornings and Jen in the afternoons. Apart from our tiny room, there was nowhere else to go. Our host family made it clear that the room was ours and the rest of the house was theirs.

Every morning after I had left for the language school, Jen would wander the streets with Katelyn, trying to occupy her mind and keep her busy. In the afternoons it would be my turn. Everyone seemed very patient with our attempts to speak Spanish.

It didn't take us long to get to know Antigua very well. I suppose it was the wandering around that we did that helped us meet people. It also meant that we came across situations we would rather have avoided.

Antigua had suffered greatly from an earthquake in its recent history. The earthquake had almost devastated the city. Today it's a thriving tourist spot because of its 'old-worldliness' of cobbled streets and ruins of churches, monasteries and grand houses, giving the visitor a glimpse of how life used to be a few hundred years ago. The peeling paintwork on nearly all the buildings reinforces the sense of antiquity.

It was nearly Christmas 1992 when we had a phone call at the language school from the *Daily Express*. They were writing an article on us and wanted some information about the apparent kidnapping of children. We'd read in the papers that a house in Antigua had been raided by police, and six babies and young children were rescued. They all had false papers and foreign adoption papers. We decided to investigate a little and ask around – starting with the local hospital.

Posing as a would-be buyer, I was informed that no babies were currently available. Then I spoke to someone who told me about a lady who ran a language school and knew of cases where children had been stolen and then sold. I went to meet her and she told me that it would be possible to buy a baby for $100,000. The Guatemalan mother would get $6,000.

The woman claimed to have evidence of one of the hospitals in the city selling children's body parts. She explained the procedure: the mother is told that her child is dead – then the child's organs are removed. She refused to say any more and just drew her fingers across her throat.

I left and went to meet Jen and Katelyn and we walked home together. Suddenly we noticed that two people were following us. They caught up with us and began to walk with us. They talked about the country and asked if we liked it there.

Then the subject changed. They started asking about Katelyn. We didn't realise that by now we had arrived outside the house where we were staying and needed to say our goodbyes.

The couple began to ask if they could hold Katelyn. We politely said that we would rather not. But the couple insisted that they needed to just hold her. A few seconds later they were trying to forcibly remove Katelyn from Jen's arms! It was all so unreal. Thank God Doña Elena, the lady we were living with, came out into the street and pulled us all inside the house, warning us of 'people who steal children'. It made us even more alert and cautious.

Two days later, Jen was walking through town when a man approached her and asked about Katelyn. He then offered Jen a sum of money to buy our daughter. Jen ran away in fear and came to me at the language school very upset.

We began to see Guatemala in a different light. We found out that a group of students from the language school had been attacked, mugged and raped. Another group of students were caught in crossfire between the Guatemalan army and a guerrilla group fairly close by. The civil war was continuing to cause problems, and we noticed an increase in the number of soldiers patrolling the streets.

One day we went for a short walk out into the country only to hear gun shots, then more heavy weapons fire. Later we saw two men in handcuffs being walked down the road by two policemen. At times like this the violence really scared us.

That month, there were more reports of abuse against street children. Four children had been taken from the streets by uniformed officers and beaten inside a police vehicle. All the children were then thrown from the vehicle while it was driving at speed. Another report told how two street children were sitting outside a market when two traders grabbed the boys and began to beat them. They justified their actions by saying the boys were responsible for a drop in sales.

Katelyn was causing us concern. She was eating very little and had lost a lot of weight. We had her checked out by a doctor. He told us to feed her some supplements and try to force food down her, as her weight was so low. I was also suffering from an upset stomach most days. It was just something you had to get used to. We would always plan our day around places we knew that had toilets.

Each week we would read the papers and send reports to England about the current political situation – and the worsening plight of the street children. We noted the following in our journal:

• A Guatemalan magazine reported that over the twelve months of 1992, 1,000 people had been found executed by the side of the road or had been tortured. As a result of this report, their offices were bombed in Guatemala City.

• A house in town was raided by police and six babies and young children rescued. These children had all been reported as stolen and were being prepared for adoption to foreign couples. One of the babies had a distinctive mark on its hand. Its mother, a prison inmate, had given birth to the baby a month previously. Prison officials had sedated the woman after the birth. When she came round she was told that her baby had died. Fortunately, mother and child were reunited.

• Two armed men grabbed a twenty-seven-year-old man in the streets and strapped a bomb to his chest. At gunpoint they ordered him to walk into a fast-food restaurant in Guatemala City. But the bomb failed to go off. Soldiers managed to deactivate it. When the police arrived, they arrested and charged the man for possessing explosives.

• A six-year-old boy was assassinated in zone nineteen of Guatemala City for no apparent reason.

• UNICEF reported that 70 per cent of all child deaths in Guatemala are a direct result of malnutrition. Out of every 1,000 children born, 300 die before they reach age two. They also reported that one of their workers had found a girl in urgent need of medical treatment tied to a tree in the countryside. Her parents thought she was going mad because she was crying out in so much pain, so they tied her to a tree and left her there for many months. The girl wasn't mad, but only in need of a small operation. UNICEF took her to hospital where she got the treatment she desperately needed. (UNICEF is the United Nations Children's Fund and has an office in Guatemala City. They have provided useful resources to the ministry over the years. They have extensive knowledge of the acute problems facing the ordinary Guatemalan and speak out for the children – who are always the innocent victims of man's sin. They were the only other agency with whom we made some contact.)

• A small boy was found dead in the streets, shot in the head. Four street children were badly beaten by police for being on the streets. One policeman poured the shoe glue the child was sniffing over his head. A nine-year-old boy was killed by a hand grenade, which also injured two of his friends, aged three and twelve.

• Over 1992 violent crime increased by 60 per cent. On average, thirty buses per day are held up at gunpoint and passengers robbed and sometimes killed.

• A street boy named Daniel was sitting in a park in Guatemala City when two men approached him and one hit him with a metal pipe. The men walked off, leaving Daniel dazed and in great pain. Daniel later collapsed and died in hospital.

News like that was a daily occurrence. We began to wonder how God's love could ever break through to Guatemala. Yet God continued to remind us that he was in control. Our job was to pray and be prepared for what he next had in mind. I sent a letter to Ian Edwards.

'We both find it very hard to live here,' I said. 'Jen is especially finding life tough and is very upset about everything. She knows God wants us here. But she finds it hard to cope with the tummy upsets and living conditions.' It was wearing us down.

After three months of language training, Jen and I were asked to run a children's home which was just outside Antigua. In the home were fifteen boys aged between five and twelve. Each child had either been abandoned or given to the home because their families could not feed them or look after them any more.

To reach the boys' home by car you would have to drive along a dry and dusty mud road, where little traffic passed. But most people got there by foot from the main road. The high walls around the home meant that inside it was safe and secure. A large unkept garden was in the centre of the property. It was bordered on three sides by a concrete path leading to bedrooms, bathrooms, store, kitchen, dining room and lounge.

A side gate at the back of the property led on to some waste ground that was owned by the charity. There the boys would happily play for hours, making camps and enjoying the freedom and security the high walls afforded. There was little noise, as the house was in a fairly quiet neighbourhood. The silence was broken by just the occasional bird or passing car. It was idyllic.

The house was in a town called Ciudad Vieja which was set at the bottom of a very large but non-active volcano. Beyond the walls, the landscape was dominated by brightly coloured plants and trees, with the traditional large red flower of those parts. From all points of the house, the view was beautiful.

Before moving into the home, lock stock and barrel, we were given accommodation 500 yards away from the boys' home. It was an opportunity to get used to running a children's home gradually while spending part of the day on further language training. Each day our Spanish teacher would go with us to the home as we got to know the children and tried to get to know the workers.

Staying with us was Dr Naomi Richman from Save the Children in London. She was training the workers on helping children in difficult circumstances. We talked with her about all we were experiencing in the boys' home and she suggested ways to improve the situation. Jenni, the dietitian, was busy looking at the organisation's menus to determine if the boys were getting a balanced diet.

The big day came. Despite all that had happened in the month leading up to our move to the home, we were excited about what God wanted to do in the boys' lives. Through the generosity of friends and family in the UK, money had been sent to us for the purchase of a small minibus. We used it to move all our worldly goods – three suitcases, a cot and a double bed.

Because of the huge increase in violence over the previous year, people using public transport were especially vulnerable. Sometimes people died as fights ensued between police and criminals or between criminals and passengers. We thought it best to have transport of our own that we could use for the children. You could never rely on anyone for transport. And the lack of it made us feel very isolated.

On our arrival at the home, the children showed their obvious excitement. They helped us unload our possessions into our room. Then everything went in slow motion. The worker who had been told to help us for the first month made it clear that she didn't want us in the home. She locked herself in her room and refused to come out or even talk to us.

The boys were already going through our things and running off with the few toys Katelyn possessed. Two of the boys had run off down the street. Two others had taken Katelyn off 'to play'. The rest were trying to set fire to the minibus.

It was a nightmare.

It took us a few hours to gather everyone together and try to restore some sense of order to the place. I am unable to go into details in this book. But what took place over the next twelve hours was very harrowing and uncomfortable.

'Just where is God in all of this?' we questioned.

The following day, we arranged an appointment with our supervisor, who invited us to another meeting to explore what could be done. We thought we were going to meet with her and discuss the options open to us and how to care for the boys effectively.

Before we spoke with her, we were invited to meet with all the other house parents and care workers in the area who were also working for the organisation. To our horror, our supervisor stood up in front of the whole group of about twenty people and explained that Duncan and

Jenni had moved into the boys' home and had found problems there.

We were asked to stand in front of the group and explain how we were feeling and why there were problems. The two workers from the home, one of whom was the person who had locked herself in her room when we moved in, were sitting on the front row.

In our best Spanish, we tried to tell of what we had seen in the previous month and how we felt about the home, the boys and the staff. We have decided not to write about specific allegations in this book. That wouldn't help anyone involved. But when we looked back over all that we witnessed in the home, we were left in a state of shock. After our emotional address, the supervisor asked for comments.

One by one, the workers got to their feet and said, 'You are not wanted here'; 'We didn't ask you to come here and anyway these things are cultural'; or 'We are Catholic and you are Evangelical and we don't need people like you working with our kids.' At the end of the meeting we felt totally alone.

'Why have we come to Guatemala, if only to suffer?' we cried out to God.

On meeting the national director the following day, it was agreed that we would leave the home and move to Guatemala City. Another opportunity was waiting for me to join the agency's street team. It was very sad leaving the home. We felt we had let everyone down, including God. We put our thoughts down in a fax to England:

We met the national director and many things were said in confidence. We outlined our growing doubts and frustrations with the organisation, and how near we feel to leaving. The director was clearly annoyed at the things we had found out and said he would look into our three-page report on all we had witnessed.

The next two days were black, literally. We were without power. The URNG, the largest guerrilla army in the country, had blown up two electricity towers in the city. President Jorge Serrano took over all the TV channels later that week to denounce the URNG. He added that within ninety days he would have a peace deal signed with them. But this was a big dream. The guerrilla army – made up mainly of peasant farmers who'd been illegally evicted from their land – was committed to continuing the war until just retribution was administered and some agrarian reform was in place.

It took us two weeks to find and rent a property in Guatemala City. A small two-bedroom house was for rent near one of the main bus routes into the centre of the city. It seemed ideal. So we snapped up the chance to have somewhere of our own.

We moved in over the weekend. We had room to park the minibus in the front yard, which Katelyn used as a football pitch. On the Monday morning, I was to start work as a volunteer street worker.

'Maybe this will be the right decision,' I thought, 'maybe this is what God had planned for us all along.'

At 7.20 a.m. I left the house and walked down to the bus stop. I assumed it was the bus stop because that was where a whole crowd of people were gathering, waving their hands at full buses that passed by. I had worked out the bus I needed and waited until one stopped. The only room left was the entrance. I held on for dear life, as more and more people squeezed into and around the bus!

Guatemala must have a deal with an American bus

company to buy the oldest vehicles possible and then paint them and turn them into part of its national transport system. The large Ford engines exhale fumes that leave behind a large black cloud.

It is customary for bus drivers to decorate their buses inside and out with religious symbols, which demonstrates how far syncretism has permeated Guatemalan culture. The signs that pronounce 'Jesus is my guide' and 'Jesus is King' hang next to pictures of naked women and New Age symbols. Every bus has a helper who collects the fares, then hangs out of the door shouting for possible customers. It is all quite an experience!

In true British fashion, I arrived at the refuge two minutes before eight o'clock.

'Hello,' I said, 'I am Duncan Dyason and I have been asked to report to the street team.' The man on the gate asked me to come in and sit in the waiting room. A short while later another man came out and asked me what I wanted.

'My name is Duncan Dyason,' I said, 'and I have been asked to report here to work with the street team.'

'Please wait here,' was his response. As he returned to the office, I could hear his conversation with his colleagues, which lasted for the next thirty minutes. The small group of people in the office were clearly not impressed that I had turned up. After a few phone calls and a general argument about what to do with me, the person returned and invited me into the office. It was like walking into the lions' den!

After a hostile reception from the street team, I was told to go with one of the workers and another volunteer to the streets. As we walked along, it was explained that we would be visiting a particularly violent group of teenagers. I was to observe and try not to get in the way.

I talked a little with John, a volunteer from Europe, who had also recently started working with the street children.

I can only describe my first day on the streets as one of the most stressful days I have ever experienced in my life – so far! We arrived at a park which was situated near the city rubbish dump. It was about 10.00 a.m. The morning sun was now quite hot and already burning the back of my neck.

The park was divided into two parts. The first was a play area for small children which included slides and climbing frames. But they were all made out of reinforced concrete! That section of the park was surrounded by a high chain-link fence. A few trees were scattered around, but it looked drab and was clearly not well maintained.

The second part of the park was a dirt football pitch with large metal goal posts. At the far end of the park you could clearly see the city dump, which gave off a constant stench. It certainly wasn't Disneyland.

I watched as the street worker greeted the children. Then he and John began to attend to the children's wounds with the first-aid kit they'd brought with them. I am quite tall anyway, and most Guatemalan adults only reach my chest. I towered over them – which made me stand out even more. So I was to spend most of each day bending over people or kneeling down. Then I could look directly into their eyes without them having to bend their necks right back in order to see my face.

I decided to pluck up courage and talk to the street children myself. I thought they would be pleased to talk to me. And I had thought of all the little things I could do to show I wanted to be their friend. The first boy ignored me. The second did the same. The third boy spat at me as though I was a dog.

'This isn't going to be easy,' I thought to myself.

The boys came to life when all their wounds had been taken care of and we produced a football. Two teams were selected, with me being the last person chosen. It was just like being back at school, really. I was amazed to see how proficient the boys were at playing football. They ran rings around me – which wasn't too difficult – and I wondered how they found the energy to keep going.

I soon found out. Now and again one of the boys would dig down into his trousers, pull out a small plastic bag or bottle of glue and take a few sniffs before continuing with the game. The few sniffs turned into a few more sniffs, which resulted in the group getting very high an hour or so later. I noticed that as the game came to an end, the boys started to become violent.

'*Vamos*,' said the street worker. That meant, 'Let's go.' He dragged me away from trying to say goodbye to the boys, and off we went. Looking back, I could see that as the three of us left the park, the boys started to follow us. They were shouting. Then they started throwing rocks at us.

'I think we'd better run,' I was told. So we ran!

I felt scared and wondered why the children were so violent towards people who were just trying to help them. As we ran across the road, the bus we needed came into sight. I felt safe again. But then, just as the bus began to pull in, the group of boys started to run across the road.

Catching sight of this rabble of street children stamped-ing across the road with rocks in their hands, the bus driver slammed his foot hard on the accelerator – and left. So we were stranded. And a mob of very angry street children was heading our way.

The children began to fight with us. Then they fought with each other. A small crowd of people began to form.

That affected the traffic flow as drivers slowed down to watch the fighting.

A motorcyclist stopped, put his bike on its stand, and began to hit some of the children. Then one of the boys picked up a paving slab and dropped it on another boy's head. The boy slumped to the ground. Two other lads kicked him as he lay limp on the pavement. A few minutes later, an ambulance arrived. But the crew took one look at the children fighting and left.

'They're only street children,' they said, as they drove away. As we tried to calm the children down, the police arrived. Two officers got out of their car. They pulled out their handguns and began to hit the children over the heads with the butts of their weapons until the youngsters were all sitting down or had run away. I stood watching, helplessly. Then I felt someone tugging at my t-shirt.

'Come on,' I was told, 'the bus is here now.' As we got on the bus, the boys who hadn't been beaten by the police were trying to get in through the back door. The bus driver pulled away and the boys were left behind. We later found out that, as we left that morning, one of the boys was shot in the back.

We returned to the office, which took up two rooms in the refuge. It was small but with high walls. The only window looked out on to the streets and, like all windows in Guatemala, had heavy-duty iron bars across it. Children would often congregate there, to ask for a plaster or some water. They were constantly knocking at the window demanding help.

Inside the office were large filing cabinets full of information and photos of the children. In some files it was possible to read the full life history of a child and look at any copies of official documents that were available for that child. Also in the room was a large medicine cabinet and a resources cupboard for paper, pencils, games, footballs, etc. It was situated on a busy and noisy street in zone one.

I was asked to write out a report of all that had happened. It was difficult to know where to begin – especially when my written Spanish wasn't that good. After writing the report and having lunch with the workers, I sat down and talked with John. He really loved being with the children. The kids loved the physical affection they were receiving from him. Then I became aware that the 'play' between John and the boys in the refuge wasn't that healthy.

As I watched John bounce one of the boys up and down on his knee, I noticed he was becoming over-affectionate. Then it happened. John's hand slid down inside the boy's trousers. I couldn't believe what I was seeing. It made me sick. So I approached another worker and explained what had happened.

Later I returned home. Jen asked me how the first day had been. I knew it would take quite a bit of explaining. The following day, John didn't turn up for work. When I asked what had happened to him, I was told they had asked him not to work with us any more.

It appeared that John hadn't been arrested and charged with abuse. I couldn't believe those steps hadn't been taken. It was obvious that he would carry on abusing children, as he had told me of his plans to visit other street children projects in Latin America. I felt angry and also upset for the little boy who'd left the streets and now felt his trust betrayed and his body abused once more.

'We're going to the hotels this morning,' I was told the next day. 'Get the first-aid kit ready. We're going to need it.' I prepared the small, basic medical kit the best way I knew how. I checked that all was clean and that there were enough plasters, bandages and cough medicine. Then we left the refuge and walked down the busy streets teeming with pedestrians, street vendors and bus fumes. The sun was hot. It made the bus fumes stick to the sweat on your skin.

We headed for zone one, downtown Guatemala City. The zones are used throughout Guatemala to identify in which district people live. The street system is based on the American layout of streets and avenues built at right angles to each other, with all the streets running in one direction and the avenues running across them. And obviously, as the city grows, new zones are added.

In zone one there is a street full of very cheap hotels. As we approached, I saw young boys and girls hanging around looking for opportunities to make some money. The children welcomed us and invited us into one of the hotels where they said a girl was ill. Child prostitution is a growing business in Guatemala. Young children sell their bodies to total strangers for sometimes as little as 20 pence.

On walking through the entrance, I wondered why the name 'hotel' was given to this rundown brothel. It was dark inside. I slipped as I walked up the stairs. At the bottom of the steps was a young girl, probably about fourteen, washing a little baby in a communal sink. The baby was screaming and looked very malnourished.

The hallway was carpeted with bits of food and rubbish. Some light broke in through a skylight window. There were sounds of shouting and crying. The noise of the streets had diminished to a background hum.

'In here,' the children said, inviting us into one of the rooms.

The two workers with me greeted the three boys and four girls who'd been sleeping in the room. Some were still in bed together, and showed no shame as they dressed and asked us to sit with them on one of the beds. A couple of cockroaches were devouring the remnants of the evening meal on the floor.

I tried to shake hands with a couple of the older boys who were walking around in just their underwear. They looked me up and down and asked the street workers who I was and what I was doing.

After a brief explanation, I sat down on one of the beds and watched as one of the workers talked with the young girl who was in need of medical attention. The girl had been stabbed in the stomach and was in great pain. She had a fever and had been too scared to go to the hospital for help.

While the workers talked with her and two of the boys, I looked around the room. There were no windows at all. The room was lit by one single light bulb. The switch for the light was just two wires hooked together by the door. The room had been painted many times with dark-coloured paint, so that each wall was a different colour. The paint was flaking off all over, revealing previous attempts at decorating.

Under one of the beds lay a pile of clothes together with various radios and other items. Later I found out those had been stolen and were going to be sold that day.

'Would you step outside for a moment?' the two older boys asked me. And, foolishly, I obliged. They pulled out a large knife and pushed it against my stomach. They stood silent for a moment.

'Now give me your wallet, passport and watch,' said one of the boys.

As I looked at their faces I could see a hardness I'd never seen in a person before. It was a kind of hardness that served to protect them. I smiled and looked into their eyes. The boy with the knife laughed and hid it away under his shirt.

'They told me to do it,' he said, 'the workers, they told me to bring you out here and scare you.'

The following weeks were much the same. Every day we'd leave the office and visit the different groups of street children. Little by little I got to know them, and discovered how the groups operated and how the different characteristics and rules changed for each group. As I began to get to know the street children, they got to know me too, and so opened their lives to me. For some that took at least two years.

One day we left the office to visit a group of children – mainly girls – who lived by prostitution in 19th Street, zone one. On leaving the office we had to walk through a group of street boys who were hanging around outside, sniffing glue. Glue is a very cheap form of drug abuse. The street children we've worked with have either started the day with glue or use it continually throughout the day. The older street youths buy it in quantity and then sell it to the younger ones in small plastic bags.

As a child exhales into the plastic bag, it warms up the glue. The vapour that's released is then inhaled by the child. Most children who abuse glue do so on a regular basis. It leaves them in a constant state of dependency which results in hallucinations, sores around the mouth and nose, declining health and, often, brain damage. But it makes them feel 'out of it'. Some of the children say it helps to take away the hunger pains or deaden all that is within them that wants to cry out for someone to care.

I've always found that whenever the children have inhaled glue, that has led to hallucinations. They experience two things. First, they hear voices. Second, they see monsters. For the children who have heard us talk about the love of Jesus Christ, those voices always tell them to forget what we have told them. The voices twist the truth they've been taught. The monsters they see in their hallucinations are always chasing them, which results in the children wandering around looking very 'spaced out'. Sometimes they are knocked down by cars or lorries when they are in that state.

So there they were, a small group of boys getting high on glue as we left the office. They looked right through us – as though we didn't exist – and continued to see and experience another world.

Within ten minutes we'd arrived at a major road intersection. On one side there was a small bus terminal which also housed a variety of *tiendas* – tin huts turned into shops. They were selling drinks, fruit and a range of other foods. In the middle of the intersection was a fly-over where a group of young girls spent their day hoping for customers to pass by and offer them 'work'.

As we approached the girls, some moved away to the other side of the road. The ones that remained began to ask for medical help. The first one I saw was a girl called Miriam. At first I guessed her age at about thirty, maybe thirty-five. I was shocked when she told me she was only sixteen.

Miriam had lived on the streets for the past three years. Her appearance told me that she had certainly suffered. There were scars all over her face and neck. She'd obviously been cut across the face at some point, and that had left a scar that was very noticeable.

'It's my feet,' she said to me.

'Go ahead,' one of the workers told me, 'clean her up.'

Nervously I opened up the medical kit and asked to see her feet. She pulled off her shoes, revealing her black swollen feet, and showed me where she thought the problem was. Both feet were infected. I felt very much out of my depth.

'You just need to clean them,' Miriam told me. So I began to clean her feet with some water and a cloth. It was all very basic. On her leg was a large scab. All around it was red.

'This as well,' she said, pointing to the scab.

I began to spray her leg with a cleaning fluid. Then I wiped it with some gauze. As the scab came off, the wound became open. The more I cleaned it, the more pus came out. A couple of minutes later the young girl had a hole in her leg that seemed to go right to the bone. There was a nasty smell. I wondered how long the infection would take to spread to her whole leg.

Out of the corner of my eye I noticed a group of teenage boys walking up to where we were. Miriam was leaning against the bonnet of a car, and I was kneeling down tending her wounds. The boys began shouting and jostling one another. One of them shouted at Miriam, then punched her right in the face. She fell back on the car bonnet and began to cry. The boy who hit her shouted at her again. It was something about not paying him money. Then he and his gang left.

Miriam was still crying and had a nose-bleed now. I passed her a tissue, and felt like chasing after the group of boys. But I saw that one of the other workers had done that, and was talking with them.

'Why?' I asked.

'For money,' she replied. 'He and his gang control this area. You have to do what they say.'

'Who is he?' I asked.

'Oh, he is the leader,' Miriam said. 'His name is Nicky Cruz.' I was astonished to think that this gang leader shared the same name as the notorious gang leader in the book *The Cross and the Switchblade*.

That day the Guatemalan newspaper *Siglo XXI* – it means twenty-first century – reported that the director of the national police was trying to co-ordinate an investigation into the street children:

> The officer produced a police study, and explained its conclusions by tearing up little pieces of paper to represent different segments of society. As if he was playing a game of chess, he moved the pieces on his desk, tracing the life of a street child. 'The child,' he said, 'lives with his family. The family doesn't have work. The father is an alcoholic. The mother is a drug addict. The child goes to live with an aunt who doesn't want the child either. The child is sent back to his parents. The child runs to the streets . . .' he said, moving bits of paper about.
>
> The officer then distinguished between two piles of crumpled paper: children who are the victims of circumstance, and criminals who happen to be children. He explained that for the first group, the national police are looking for ways to encourage families to reclaim responsibility. And for delinquents, he believes the national police and the juvenile court system must be allowed to do their job with co-operation, not interference, from human rights organisations.

The following day we visited the city rubbish dump where hundreds of garbage pickers live. Men, women and children work on top of the swamp of steamy refuse, ferreting around for pieces of glass, plastic or paper for resale. The dump's overwhelming stench permeated our skin and clothing. When we got back into the minibus

Katelyn kept saying, 'Dirty, smelly, dirty,' as she brushed invisible dust off her legs and hands – even though she'd been held in Jen's arms the whole time!

Children are born on the dump. Families live in rooms carved out of the rubbish. And each year, people die when they are accidentally buried alive.

Behind Guatemala's largest bus terminal is a notorious dusty alley called El Hoyo – 'The Hole' – where a large group of children live. For them, this is their home. As we entered El Hoyo, a boy pulled himself up from the crumbling pavement. He came up to us scratching his head with dirty fists and asked us for help. I don't remember his name. But he was about nine, and noticeably small for his age.

One of the staff put on some rubber gloves and gave me a pair. She asked me to look in his hair and find out what the problem was. It was hard to see the cuts on his head for all his hair. I was told I would have to cut it off. As I did so, he flinched. I noticed that he had a large cut on his head. It was a machete wound.

As I cleaned it, the scab came off and a whole army of maggots emerged from within the wound. The boy was in great pain, and I realised how important the first-aid work was for the children. They had no one else to help them if they got sick or needed a wound cleaned. We were all they had.

There is no real healthcare available to the youngsters. Poor people see healthcare as a luxury they cannot afford. Only when they are very sick can they go to the hospital emergency unit and join the long queue. Any medicine needed has to be bought by the person seeking help.

After we finished with that boy, I wandered over to where the other staff were. Word had spread that the street team had arrived and children began to flood into the alley.

They all looked undernourished as they gathered around the team. By now they were all sitting down on the side of the road, and the children were colouring in some pictures we had given them.

Now and again the children would pull their bags of glue to their noses and mouths and inhale deeply. It was then that I noticed a boy, aged about fourteen, sitting on his own watching everyone else. There was something about his face that was familiar. And then I remembered the television programme Jen and I had seen in the UK.

His name was Jose Antonio, and his story had been featured in the BBC programme. He had been walking along the road one day when a policeman pulled out a gun and shot him in the chest and stomach. He had managed to carry on walking for some time, and I remember the words he said in the television interview as he told his story. He was asked what happened and as he was describing the incident, he looked up at the interviewer and said, 'But I didn't cry.'

'Hi, my name is Duncan,' I said, as I sat down next to the lad. He looked at me and then looked down at the ground.

'I know you,' I said, 'I have seen you on television in England.' That got his attention. He asked me how I had seen him.

'You were being interviewed about the time you had been shot by the police,' I said to him. 'I remember you had scars on your chest and back from the shooting.' He lifted up his shirt. Sure enough, there were the scars.

'It was because of that programme that my wife and I came here to help you and the other street children,' I added. 'Did you know that there are many people in England who really care about the street children?'

'No one cares about us,' he said, and stood up. A whole

stream of abusive words streamed from his mouth as he told me, in no uncertain terms, how he felt, being on the streets, and that he knew no one cared. Then he walked off, but a short time later, he returned and sat down next to me.

'Do people really care?' he asked me.

'Yes,' I responded, 'I know there are many people who care. They write to us and send us money so that we can help you.' He put his head on my shoulder, as my comments sank in.

'Wait there,' he shouted, as he ran off again. When he returned he asked me to put out my arm, which I did.

'I have made this for you,' he said, tying a *pulsera* or friendship band on my wrist. 'Please wear it always and don't forget me.' Then he added, 'Whatever you do, don't forget us.'

It was a moving moment – certainly one I will never forget.

It is impossible to comprehend what it must be like to find yourself living on the streets of the city at six years of age, without security, love or food. When these desperate youngsters find another lost soul with whom they can share their lives, a close bond develops between them. If they have a means by which they can earn money to feed themselves, then they need never again trust another adult.

There was a cholera epidemic hitting Guatemala and the death toll was rising each week. Those particularly at risk were the poor, who have little or no access to clean water, and the street children. Many children were sick and were suffering from diarrhoea. So it was vital that we reach as many children as possible and teach them about the risks of cholera – and what to do if they got it.

On our return to the office, there were two street boys

waiting to see us. They said they were scared for their lives and in need of help. At 1.00 a.m. the previous night they and one other boy were walking past a hotel in zone one when two national policemen drove past in a patrol car, stopped and got out.

They asked for the boys' papers, stole forty-five Quetzales (the Guatemalan currency) from them – and their shoes – and then pushed them into the back of the patrol car. The policemen drove the boys to the cemetery and threatened them. One of the boys was held down and burned with lighted cigarettes. There was little we could do apart from file yet another report to the Human Rights office.

The organisation we had been working with since our arrival in Guatemala was causing us concern. Our time with the agency in the children's home had not worked at all. We were later told that we were just an experiment as a foreign family caring for the home, and that they had known it wouldn't work.

My time as a street worker was exciting but very demanding. Amazingly, after a very difficult start the staff had grown to like me and I felt that I was having some positive input into the work. But still I was not allowed to speak about the love of Jesus with the street children.

We found ourselves in the middle of an internal war between the workers – and we were encouraged to take sides. Time and resources were being poured into the in-fighting, which was resulting in staff being sacked. A union was established to help workers fight for their cause within the organisation.

A demonstration was held outside the central office and workers shouted for the management to resign. The walls of the central office were sprayed with intimidating graffiti. Even the Guatemalan press reported the organisation's internal struggles. Staff and volunteers came and went, issuing various complaints. It seemed as if the cause of the street children was being lost amid internal squabbles.

One night during this time, Jen and I were sitting down in our lounge when the room began to shake, then everything began to rotate. It was a peculiar feeling being in the middle of a serious earth tremor. Four people were later reported to have died during those few seconds.

Right in the middle of all this, the Guatemalan government was thrown into chaos and then into a coup. The President fled the country. The following morning we woke up to find the military in charge, and the streets full of soldiers and tanks. The coup was over within days – a counter-coup followed, and everything was returned to normal. But the President had gone. Over the weekend there were major raids in the city centre. No fewer than 1,200 prostitutes were arrested – of whom 39 per cent were minors.

After months of continuing problems and worsening health, Jen and I questioned what good we were doing in Guatemala. Why had God called us to serve him in this way? In August 1993, nearly a year after our arrival in Guatemala, we had made up our minds to leave the organisation and seek God about what he wanted us to do now. The past twelve months had been the most difficult and challenging ever – and we really needed to confirm that Guatemala was the place God wanted us to serve him.

As we reminded ourselves of the calling God had upon our lives, and how he had revealed his will to us, we wondered what to do next. We needed every bit of confirmation God had given us up to this point to persevere with our calling to demonstrate God's love to the street children of Guatemala. I prayed and told God that I had nothing else to give him. My emotions were shot. My health had deteriorated. My walk with him was not that good, and there was nothing else I felt I could do.

'Good. Now let me live through you,' I felt God say to me. 'For when you are weak, I can be strong.'

We handed in our notice to the organisation. That was a very hard thing to do. I was suffering from constant stomach cramps and was diagnosed as having giardiasis. I took some time out to rest. Most days I had just enough strength to walk between the bedroom and the toilet.

Jen felt alone and depressed and very afraid and came in to talk to me, but I was asleep. She wished she could pick up the phone and talk to someone, but knew the call would cost too much money and so sat down, picked up her Bible and began to read John's gospel. When she got to John 14:27, God spoke to her powerfully about her situation and how she was to trust him alone: 'Peace I leave with you; my peace I give you. I do not give to you as the world gives. Do not let your hearts be troubled and do not be afraid.' Jen knew this was of God, as he was teaching her a valuable lesson.

It was at that time that Cath Grant tried to phone Jen but, as we found out later, couldn't get through. We had known Cath from church. She and her children were regular members, although her husband Gary never came. Back home, I'd given my testimony at an outreach event one evening, which included a humorous mime of a burglar's attempt to break into a house whereupon he became locked in the safe.

Cath had brought Gary to the meeting and he was challenged. God had begun something in his life. He became a Christian while attending another church the following Sunday. Before we left for Guatemala Gary and

Cath invited us round and said they wanted to support us in prayer. They'd been faithful in writing letters and sending little gifts through to encourage us.

Not being able to speak to us, Cath then wrote, saying that she felt God had a word for us. It came from Genesis 28:15: 'I am with you and will watch over you wherever you go, and I will bring you back to this land. I will not leave you until I have done what I have promised you.' Her husband Gary also wrote and felt that we needed to read Psalm 25 – which really encouraged us.

'These verses helped us cope and to trust God to carry on here,' said our diary entry for that day.

7

The Toybox Opens Up

It was the autumn of 1994 and I was busy working in our office when a boy came rushing upstairs. There was obviously something serious or urgent on his mind.

'Duncan,' he called out, 'come and have a look at this.' I emerged from the office and accompanied the sixteen-year-old lad, Caesar, downstairs. He led me into the kitchen.

'Look,' he exclaimed, 'you mix this stuff together and put it in the oven.' He proceeded to show me – in great detail – how he had been taught to bake biscuits. He was amazed that you could mix together flour, butter and sugar, roll the mixture out on the table, cut it into shapes, place the shapes on a tray and then place it in the oven.

After fifteen minutes we took the biscuits out of the oven and they were ready for eating. He was so impressed!

'Duncan, I could be a baker,' he said. His words rang in my ears as I thought that here was a young man who previously had no hope for tomorrow. He never spoke of his desires for the future, and just like all the other street children, only thought of what was immediate in his life. So his words, 'I could be a baker,' encouraged me. For that moment, we had helped him see that he could be someone.

'Why doesn't God remove all the pain in the world?' people often ask me.

There are no easy answers – except to think that what we are really asking of God is to remove all the suffering from life. When you explain the consequences of God actually doing such a thing, people tend to rethink things and only want God to intervene in situations that they think appropriate. God doesn't always help us remove the pain. But he does help us restore the hope. Caesar had his hope restored that day. I pray what began that day will produce fruit in his life one day – or, should I say, produce cakes!

Caesar was one of the first successes at our new training centre. That, too, was born out of tears. We had met with our pastor, Daniel Johnson. He prayed for us to know God's guiding hand. Daniel, an American missionary, was co-pastor of the small church that met near our home and where each week I went with Jen and Katelyn. It was amazing the way God brought Daniel to us and through him the first Toybox workers.

Our gas boiler had gone wrong – again – and we phoned the company who had installed it. A couple of days later an engineer came to fix it and began talking with Jen about his church. He needed to return to our home a few days later, as the problems persisted, and told us more about his church.

He encouraged us to share our vision for helping the street children with the church on Sunday. We expected nothing. In fact we were thinking of returning to the UK as nothing had worked out in Guatemala since we had put our feet on Guatemalan soil.

Sunday morning came. I was panicking about having to stand up in front of the church and talk about our vision for the street children – in Spanish! It wasn't as bad an experience as I thought it might be. The pastor encouraged everyone to come to the church the following evening and pray with me about the street children.

I arrived at the church early to set out the chairs and prepare for the prayer meeting. I thought it best to share something of God's heart for the lost and for the children, and to pray for his will to be done. I was so disappointed that only two people came to the meeting.

The following Sunday, the pastor took to the stage and invited people again to meet with me in order to pray about starting a ministry to street children. You could see the way the words 'street children' were received by people – with fear, hatred, mistrust and indifference. But a week later we saw a 50 per cent increase in numbers, as three people came!

After a time of prayer and worship I invited the three people to come with me on to the streets and meet some of the children. They weren't expecting to actually go out – just pray about it. I tried to explain to them, as they were leaving the building for home, that God calls us to put our faith and prayers into action.

I think they must have thought that I was just a crazy gringo who wanted to save Guatemala, and if they went with me this once I would see for myself that these children were just common thieves and should be treated as such – and not with a hug and a smile.

We walked for about ten minutes and arrived at El Hoyo. The alley divided the brothels on one side from the sordid clubs and bars on the other. All offered sex for sale at an affordable price to the young men who frequented the area. El Hoyo was often raided by police and army security patrols. Such raids achieved nothing. Most residents told me they just had to pay the police a sum of money and nothing else would be said.

I remember standing outside one of the brothels talking with a group of street children. The brothel had just been raided, and the police hadn't arrested anyone. Just then a policeman came staggering out while trying to zip up his trousers! Obviously a deal had been made. As we entered El Hoyo, a young street boy came running up to me and gave me a hug. He looked at Alex, one of the church volunteers.

'Who are you?' the lad asked.

'Hello, my name is Alex,' my colleague replied. The child shook his hand and asked him why he was in El Hoyo. I listened to Alex's response as he tried to explain that he was going to work with me and help the street children. The young boy looked at him.

'Yes, but for how long?' he said. Then he walked off into the shadows.

We stood still and thought about what the boy had said. It was obvious to me that he had been used to people coming and going all the time. No one stayed, they all came, saw the 'poor little children' – and then left. I was determined that if we began a Christian ministry among these children, it would be with nationals – people who could commit themselves to these children for the long term.

It was a difficult night. The alley was filled with young men standing around in small groups. The bars were playing their music at its usual full volume. There was dancing, and drinking. Upstairs the business of sex went on. Many street children were huddled together in a group getting high on glue.

We approached the group and sat down in front of them. As we began to talk to the children, it was obvious that the two volunteers with me had little idea of how these children lived and why they were on the streets. After a couple of hours of talking with the children we told them we'd come back next week.

'Can you bring a football?' one boy asked.

'I'll do my best,' I replied, as we began to leave. Some children walked with us a couple of blocks until they said goodbye and returned to their night on the streets. Alex suggested that we return the following week with our Bibles and a guitar.

'It would be good to teach them some Bible stories and preach to them,' he said.

I felt torn in two. Many months before, I had talked with a group of street children about Christianity and their perceptions of church. In Guatemala you're either Catholic or Evangelical. There are other religious groups and cults, but these are few and are rarely seen on the streets – especially in places like El Hoyo.

The children discussed among themselves where they felt their allegiances lay. Most said they were Catholic, but had probably only ever been inside a church once in their lives – if that. When the discussion changed to that of the Evangelical Church, I tried to make a mental note of their comments.

'It's like this,' explained one boy, 'the Evangelicals are the ones that come to the parks and preach at us.'

'What do you mean, they preach at you?' I asked.

'Well, they come with a black Bible and preach long sermons. Sometimes they come in groups and have a microphone and loudspeakers. They always ask you, after their sermon, to go forward or stand up and pray a prayer asking Jesus into your life.'

I was excited. The church was active in the city! All along I had thought that the Evangelical Church remained within their buildings and didn't reach out to those who lived on the streets.

'So have you ever said that prayer?' I asked the group.

'Oh yes,' most of them replied, 'we say it quite often.'

'If you say the prayer,' one boy explained, 'then they get all excited and give you a hug. Some groups will give you something to eat or maybe some clothes when you have said the prayer.'

I was beginning to realise that the children weren't responding to God and his love. They were responding to their own need for a hug, some food and maybe the offer of clothes.

'I go forward every time,' a small boy added, 'and sometimes I cry for them because I know they like it.' His words struck my heart and I cried inside.

All this rushed through my mind when Alex suggested taking our Bibles and a guitar. For the moment, I thought it was best that we just tried to get to know the children before 'evangelising' them. The words 'demonstrating God's love' came to my mind.

I knew we needed to demonstrate the love of God to these children in a practical way. They were so used to Christians coming and expecting a certain response from them that they had responded by trying to manipulate the situation for their own ends. They had become very good at that. And it had kept them alive.

On returning to the church, we prayed. I felt some verses from Isaiah come to my mind. I turned to them and read the following: 'You have been a refuge for the poor, a refuge for the needy in his distress, a shelter from the storm and a shade from the heat' (Isaiah 25:4). As I shared those verses, we felt God was saying to us that this was something we needed to be for the children so they could know God's love in their lives.

A picture of a castle came to my mind. I felt God show me that the castle represented him, like the refuge God was for his people in Isaiah 25. Historically, a castle was a place of security where people could live together in safety. When you lived inside a castle you felt secure. All your needs were met and you could rely on others to help you as they were always nearby. Once inside a castle, you could climb the tower and get a better perspective on the land and people around you.

'If only we could be a castle to the street children,' I thought. 'If only we could model that every time we were with them. Then they might know the provision of God, the security of his love – and the opportunity of seeing their life from a different perspective.'

After more prayer we felt that God might be calling us to begin a Christian ministry to street children. And so, in September 1993, we decided to go to the streets each week and visit the children. We called ourselves El Castillo. It means 'The Castle'.

The following week two volunteers, Herbert and Mauricio, came with me to visit the children. We took with us a football, as we had promised the children, and a basic first-aid kit. It only took a few minutes for the street to fill with excited children ready to play football. There's little time for play in the crazy world of the street children. But like their counterparts the world over, even they are seldom found without a smile on their young faces.

Football is the national game. It's extremely popular in Guatemala. Most people either participate in or watch a game over the weekend. And just as legendary British players have emerged from the impoverished backstreets of Manchester or London's East End, so these lads also see the game as a potential means of escaping from their situation. One boy, ten-year-old Henry, ran towards me and gave me a hug.

'I want to be on your team,' he said. First we needed to find something for goal posts. The children found tyres, bits of wood and some rocks. They made quite interesting goal posts in the road, which was now quiet as the market had closed for the night.

When we started to play, Henry came to me and took my hand. It was obvious he'd been starved of love. But I felt awkward playing football and holding his hand at the same time! Whenever I let my grip go, Henry would grab hold of one side of me or the other.

After a while I noticed a young guy sitting at the side of the road with his head in his hands. I went to him, knelt beside him and gently lifted up his head. When I did so, I noticed that he'd tried to cut his wrist.

Horrified, I called to Herbert and Mauricio, one of whom had the first-aid kit. I began to try and clean the young man's wound, but was constantly interrupted by Henry, who pulled at my shirt while calling me to play football. Looking back on the incident, I know now that Henry was seeking my attention.

He was obviously jealous that someone else was getting treatment and he wasn't. As he continued to pester me, I told him that the young man was in greater need. Henry responded by placing his head between the young man's wound and my face.

'Come on, Duncan,' he said, 'let's go and play football.'

I can't remember what I said to Henry at that point, but it was obviously out of my anger – something like 'get lost'. A few minutes later I'd finished bandaging up the young man's wrist and began to look around for Henry. He was gone. I felt very upset as I knew he only wanted to be with me and that someone else had taken his place of importance in my life.

'Come on, let's go,' I said to Herbert and Mauricio. We said goodnight to the children, collected the football and began to walk back to the church. To my joy, I saw Henry. He was sitting at the side of the road a little further up from where we had been playing football.

'Now I can say sorry,' I thought to myself. But as we got closer to Henry, I could see what he was doing. He had found a Coke bottle, had broken it and was cutting his wrist with a piece of broken glass. No amount of words could have helped in that situation. Henry only wanted to be my friend and to capture my attention. But he'd found himself in a situation where he had to compete for it. I still feel bad about that and wish that I could have reacted differently. We bandaged up Henry's wounds with tears, as we realised why he had reacted in that way.

Each week we were able to help more children. As time passed by, we increased the number of nights we visited the youngsters on the streets. One such evening, we found Oscar crying in agony because one of his gang, nine-year-old Julio, had thrown solvent into his eyes. A volunteer and I rushed Oscar to a nearby hospital where we pressured them to attend to him urgently. As the doctor began to wash out Oscar's eyes, we were asked to leave.

Guatemalan hospitals generally operate on incredibly low budgets. As a result, they can offer only basic care. All medicines have to be purchased by the patient. Hospitals are usually clean but in very bad condition, with paint peeling off the walls, beds constantly smelling of urine, and patients begging both inside and outside the wards. A feeling of hopelessness hangs over such places.

We returned to the streets where we'd left two other volunteers working with the children. Then we found out that while we were at the hospital, Julio had been arrested by the police. Another street child said that as Julio was arrested, he was beaten quite severely by one of the policemen. The incident was witnessed by the two volunteers, who hadn't known what to do. We went immediately to the police station, which measured about four metres by four metres, and asked to see a senior officer.

We explained how two of our company had watched a policeman beating a street child. We even had the number of his badge. The senior policeman asked to see the piece of paper where we'd written down the badge number. He then checked the records and said that the boy had been arrested for stealing. We asked about the policeman who hit the boy.

'What policeman?' he replied. 'What is his badge number?'. Then he threw the piece of paper in the bin, threatened us and told us we were wasting our time helping 'scum kids like these'. The following day we had to make an official complaint at the legal aid office in town. But nothing was taken any further, just like the hundreds of other alleged cases outstanding against the police and security forces for abuse of street children.

Oscar was released from hospital later that day, his red eyes evidence of the pain he'd gone through that night. Julio returned to the streets about three months later with a serious and permanent limp.

All police carry guns or rifles. Most officers are arrogant and unhelpful – especially with regard to street children. But I've also learned to look at the situation from their point of view.

'You see this child on the streets,' one policeman told me, 'he has just stolen from a market stall. So I arrest him and take him to a judge. Two days later he is back on the streets. He maybe steals a lady's handbag, I catch him and take him again to the judge. But at the end of the week he is back again on the streets. Next time I find him stealing I'm going to hit him rather than taking him to the judge. The more he steals, the more I'm going to hit him.'

It was quite clear what he was saying. The beatings get

worse each time. One day, the summary punishment ends in death. The police are frustrated with the system. More recently, some officers have actually approached me in the street and congratulated me for my efforts. That would have been unheard of two or three years ago.

After talks with the church leadership, it was agreed to open a club for the street children on the church premises once a week. A meeting was arranged where we discussed what running a youth club was all about and what was needed before we opened. By this time our loyal team of three had grown to ten.

I felt we should set a date in our calendars for the opening, and ask God to provide all that we needed. Someone suggested that it was best to do it the other way round and that as soon as we had all the equipment – which wasn't much – we could start. I had never lived like that in my relationship with Jesus. It was always a case of knowing and discerning God's will, then going for it and trusting God to provide everything necessary.

So a date was set for two weeks later. And we prayed and sought God's provision for all we needed. By the day we opened the club, we had been given all the essentials. In the UK, young people had raised money through a project called Christmas Cracker for street children around the world.

The Cracker organisation heard of our new ministry and sent us £5,000 – which helped us start up the club. As well as some wood to build a store room and office, we bought a TV set and video, plates, cups and general kitchen items, table games, food storage bins, tables and chairs.

We opened to the cheers of about thirty street children. They had all been waiting outside in the rain, and we were aware that the children were very wet. But their enthusiasm was high as they rushed up the stairs and checked out every room, window and cupboard. Some of the church volunteers looked horrified and wondered what was going to happen to their lovely church building.

On one of our first evenings, a young boy called Abelino arrived at the entrance and waited in line to come in. It was our custom that if the children wanted to come in they must allow us to search them. We had to look for drugs or weapons.

On searching ten-year-old Abelino, I found a small quantity of drugs on him. Most of the boys hid drugs in either their socks or their underwear. Searching them was a very embarrassing – but necessary – experience. I explained the rules again to Abelino, and told him he could not be invited in if he had drugs on him.

He started to shout at me and then became violent. He was so violent that Alex and I had to physically restrain him from causing us and himself damage. We took him outside the church and put him down in the street, hoping he would calm down. Alex suggested he stay with Abelino just in case he continued to be violent.

As I left and returned inside the church, Abelino walked up and down the road outside cursing, and swearing at us all. Then he found a large rock in the road. He picked it up and stood in front of Alex.

'Get out of the way,' he called to Alex, 'I'm going to smash your door down – and then all the windows.' The door of the church was plate glass and very expensive to replace. But Alex moved out of the way.

'Okay,' he said to Abelino, 'if that's what you want to do, then go ahead and smash the door. But before you do, I want you to listen to just one thing. I know how your life is on the streets. I know that if you do bad, something bad happens to you. You shout at someone, someone will then shout at you. You kick someone, someone will kick

Duncan and Jenni with daughter Katelyn.

Despite their smiling faces, these children with Duncan
are categorised as 'high risk'.

A typical slum street in Guatemala City with makeshift homes of corrugated tin.

Children in the slums of Guatemala City.

This young man is sniffing solvent: one of the few ways he can forget his troubles.

A child with no hope in his eyes.

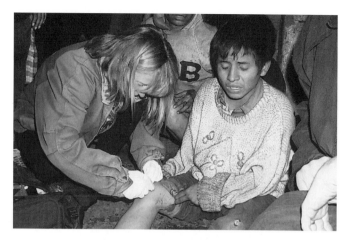

Bringing healing to the streets: without medical attention
this wound would become infected.

Duncan teaching street children to
read and write.

Children from the Boys' Home.

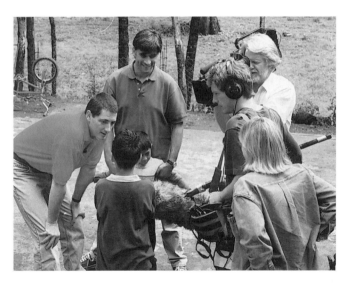

Steve Chalke, Duncan and the camera crew
from BBC's *Songs of Praise* talking to children from the
Boys' Home: November 1997.

Duncan with Byron.

Shot in cold blood by a policeman: the body of Daniel,
a street child, lies here.

Duncan with Victor (left) and Moses.

Duncan with Chiqui.

Marleny in the Girls' Home.

Many of the children who risk ending up on the streets are very young and vulnerable, like these girls.

you. So you would expect that after you have broken our door, I will come after you and beat you.'

'Well, I can run faster than you,' Abelino shouted back.

'But that's not the point,' said Alex. 'That is what you would expect me to do. Well, I am a Christian, and I know that God loves me and that he loves you too. So as soon as you break our door, I'm going to love you. In fact every time I see you I am going to try and love you more.'

Abelino couldn't believe his ears. As soon as he heard Alex's words, he burst into tears. He dropped the rock down in the road, threw away his drugs and gave Alex a big hug and asked for forgiveness. That young boy has never been a problem to us since that moment. God had begun to change his heart – and the change was evident.

Each week volunteers from the church arrived and helped prepare for youth club. We had to stack up the benches, set out tables and chairs, prepare and cook food and make sure we had enough towels, soap and medical supplies for the evening. The showers were the highlight of the evening for the children, who could wash with clean water and change their clothes for clean ones.

We operated an exchange scheme with clothes, washing their clothes each week and recycling them for the following week. Quite often the clothes had to be thrown away because they were so filthy or covered in glue. Each club night I would take home three or four large sackfuls of clothes for Jen to wash. It was the highlight of her week!

We wondered why our house was always full of fleas. Then we figured out that the fleas always multiplied whenever I brought a bag of clothes home to wash. The children's clothes came home covered in little fleas that enjoyed tucking into some white flesh. Their bites left a clear bubble on your skin which was very itchy. A few days later the bubble would burst and the bite became infected. It was not an experience I want to relive again. So we learned to spray the clothes before bringing them home, which made life a little more comfortable each week.

The club was very successful. Each week about thirty to forty children attended. We had plans for extending the club to two evenings a week, and one afternoon. If we could find volunteers for an afternoon club, we could offer the opportunity to a group of girls we were working with.

I felt particularly sad for the girls. They always seemed to have the worst deal on the streets. Not only were they suffering in every conceivable way just like their male counterparts, but also they were being abused, raped and beaten by the boys themselves.

One of the things I wanted to do for the girls was to have a club specially for them, a place where they could feel safe and which they could make their own. My dream was to invite them to a meal. We could give them the opportunity to have a shower, change into beautiful dresses, have someone to do their hair and nails – and then come with us to a fancy restaurant. I thought the evening would give the girls a view of how life could be for them and restore something of the dignity that had been taken from them.

A few weeks later, enough volunteers had offered their services, which meant that we were able to begin the afternoon club. We started with a big event, as it was one of the girls' birthdays. A full celebration was held – which included a cake, games, a present and, of course, the *piñata*.

Piñatas are a very popular and most essential ingredient to any Guatemalan party. The brightly coloured papier-mâché figure is filled with small sweets and hung up on a rope across the room. The birthday person is blindfolded and given a stick. They then try to hit the *piñata* with the stick as hard as they can to get to the sweets, while others try to pull it up and down the rope. It's hilarious to watch – and great fun!

The best part of the party was just sitting back for a moment to watch the girls enjoying themselves. For a brief moment they had forgotten all about their lives on the streets and were finding out what childhood was really all about. It was a moving experience.

After a few months of building up relationships with a group of girls, they came along to the club. Two of them had little children with them. Jen would be responsible for making sure all the girls had a shower and changed their clothes. I was responsible for food and drinks.

No sooner had the girls began to wash when Jen came up the stairs from the basement – where we'd set up the makeshift shower – saying that we needed to call the doctor. At that time, a doctor, David Estrada, was a member of our church. He would come to the club and give first-aid training for the staff. David gave his time free if we ever needed him – which we did on a regular basis.

Susa, who is the daughter of a street girl, was obviously ill and needed medical help. The doctor came and examined her, and asked us to take her to hospital, which we did. Susa needed a series of injections and had go back on a regular basis to continue treatment. As we left the hospital, the doctor called us on one side and thanked us.

'If you hadn't brought her here today,' he said, 'I think she would've been dead in a month or so.'

We found out that Susa had varying forms of sexual disease. She had been raped repeatedly. At one point, both she and her mum were held captive for a week and raped at knife-point. It really broke my heart to see little Susa in that state, and she was only two years old! Seeing her sad little face would make anyone cry.

Susa would come each week to the club with her mum, Mirna. The very first club meeting they came to, Susa sat at the feet of her mum while she talked to one of the staff. At one point Susa got up and began to walk away from her mum's side. Without hesitation Mirna reached out her hand and hit Susa round the head.

'Get back here!' she shouted as Susa began to cry. Susa walked back and sat down next to her mum. I learned that, in order to survive on the streets, babies and young children are not permitted to wander from their mother's side. Living and sleeping so close to the road means that one lapse of concentration by the mother could result in a dead child.

My daughter Katelyn was a real breakthrough in working with the girls. During an afternoon club, the girls were sitting talking. Susa was sitting on the floor by her mum as usual. Slowly, Katelyn approached Susa and sat down near her. She began to play with a little ball and rolled it to Susa, who looked suspiciously at it, picked it up, looked up at her mum, then rolled it back.

That went on for several minutes as Susa's distrust and suspicion subsided. Within the hour the two girls were running around the hall enjoying each other's company – with the approval of Mirna. There were so many things that I had taken for granted with Katelyn. Seeing the way that Susa knew nothing of how or what to play made me realise just how robbed these children are of normal childhood experiences.

The club had its ups and downs. We were able to meet the immediate needs of about sixty children each week.

But we always felt frustrated at not having anywhere for the kids to sleep. Most of the opposition we faced actually came from within the church.

A few weeks after the club opened we had to throw two boys out for smuggling in drugs and threatening staff. The boys remained outside the church hall, shouting threats and making obscene gestures to passers-by. Then I heard a smash. The boys had thrown a brick through the entrance door and one of the large side windows, and then had run away.

I ran downstairs to find the front door completely broken and glass everywhere. We decided to gather the remaining children together and explain that we weren't going to put up with such behaviour from them. As a result, we were going to close the club down for two weeks. The children started to complain and said that we'd be in trouble if they ever saw us out in the streets. They left shouting and obviously hurting. But there was little else we could do in the situation. The balance between love and justice is a delicate one and I knew the children would find it hard to accept our actions, but we knew that they had to understand that however much we loved them there were obvious limits to our acceptance of their behaviour.

We swept up the glass. I had to sleep in the church that evening – which wasn't easy as the false ceiling was infested with rats. All night long I heard them running up and down above my head – sometimes around the church, too! The church members weren't too impressed with the damage, and received a warning from the landlord. He'd had complaints from neighbours because the children hung around outside at all hours of the day and night.

Various people questioned whether we should actually be doing this type of work. After all, these were street kids, regarded by most as scum. They didn't feel this was the sort of thing the church should be doing. But the pastor decided to let us continue using the building – so long as we repaired any damage and kept it looking nice for Sundays.

We had learned to look for the negative situations around us, then go into those situations and be the positive force. So if the children were lonely, which was the negative, we would be with them, the positive. If a child was hungry, the negative, we would feed him, the positive. Jesus was always the positive in the negative world around him.

It was 10.00 a.m., Sunday. Jen, Katelyn and I walked into church. The service was scheduled to begin at 10 a.m. but rarely was anyone there at that time. Most people arrived between 10.30 and 11.00 a.m. As we walked up the stairs, a concerned-looking church elder met us and informed us that a group of street children were upstairs waiting for me. He wanted them to wait outside in the street, but the children were 'actually sitting in the church pews'. The children – all boys – stood up and greeted us with hugs and handshakes.

'We thought we would come,' they said, motioning me to sit down with them. I did so, and began to chat with them as the service began. A family came in and sat next to the children. Then they noticed they were 'Duncan's street children', so they got up and moved to the other side of the hall. I felt sad that even here in the church, the children were rejected.

The meetings were usually Pentecostal by nature, with lots of loud music and choruses which were repeated countless times. All the songs were from either the USA or Mexico. This particular service was open to families, and most people came as a family group.

It seemed that spirituality was always judged on how loud and long you prayed as well as how deeply involved you were in the worship, clapping, shouting and dancing. Not surprisingly, the boys found all that hard going.

After the first thirty minutes of worship they got up and walked around at the back. Some went into the toilets, while others went downstairs in search of food. Before long they were all escorted back by church members and sat next to me, Jen and Katelyn again.

The church notices followed the worship time. Astonishingly, members were told not to let their youngsters use the toilets today because the street children had used them – and if they did they might get AIDS!

It was hard to convince the children to return the following Sunday as news of the boys' experiences was relayed to the rest of the group. Not once did the children ever reject the idea of God. Their main problem was with the idea of church.

The relationship between the church and the children never improved. It had always been my approach that if you couldn't invite the children to church, you then took the church to the children. I knew that would come in time. But the waiting was so hard and would often leave me shouting out to God for all the things and people we needed to help these children – now!

We have tried our best to educate churches so they can receive street children. But sadly, we have a long road to travel before the established Church in Guatemala takes seriously the needs of outsiders and begins to think differently about the way it evaluates the effectiveness of its outreach.

There is much to be done before churches will be ready to accept street children. But usually the poorer churches are more open to receive these kids. However, they then target them with strict codes of conduct which are impossible to keep. It is a matter of being set free from the law and living under the grace of God.

The street children complained each week of abuses they'd suffered from the security forces. Sometimes the abuse came from people they looked up to and regarded as friends. Whenever a gringo appeared on the streets, the children assumed they were there to give them presents.

A Canadian man was seen close to El Hoyo one evening, and was asking some of the boys how much it would cost for sex. One of the boys woke up in the middle of the night to find that, as he slept on the streets, a man was raping him. The Canadian was suspected.

So we began to investigate, tracing his steps back to a hotel in zone one. We found out his name and passport number and reported that to the authorities. But the man went into hiding and was never heard of again. We also heard that eleven-year-old Carlos was rushed to hospital because someone had poured an inflammable liquid over him while he slept in front of the National Palace, and then set him alight for no apparent reason.

Christmas came around and we looked back on three fairly successful months of street work once a week and youth clubs two nights a week and one afternoon. The volunteers from the church and I looked back at all that God had done during those three months and how he had used us to demonstrate his love to many street children.

We were planning a Christmas party. The volunteers became busy preparing food, games and a little present for each child. Since our first day in Guatemala the British Embassy had been fairly sceptical about our reasons for moving there, especially since we were working with street children. Most of the time the embassy staff were helpful and supportive. The ambassador, however, made it clear that he had little interest in the plight of these children.

His official responses to letters, from us and from supporters in the UK, revealed that he had nothing constructive to say about the fact that an estimated 1,500 children slept on the streets – and a good number of those within two miles of his embassy. But when we started our independent work among the street kids, the ambassador took a keen interest in our little club.

I invited him along, thinking that he would probably refuse. But it was worth a try. Surprisingly, he said he would visit. It wasn't far for him to come as the club was literally just the other side of the road from the embassy.

A large white Range Rover pulled up outside the club and two bodyguards got out and checked around the car. One opened the back door, and the ambassador stepped out and walked into the club. I introduced him to the volunteers and to some of the children. The ambassador spoke Spanish and began to talk to the children.

At all times his bodyguards kept very close to him. I could see that, as he spoke to the children, his face lit up and his heart warmed towards them. 'But they are just children,' he said to me. After about half an hour he left. The following week he called me to the embassy.

'I want to help you,' he said. 'What do you need?' It just so happened that I had a list of items in my pocket – so I gave it to him! 'Okay,' he said with a smile, 'we're going to buy you a new cooker and fridge-freezer. Just go out and choose what you need and tell me how much it will all cost.'

I left the embassy thanking God for the way he'd granted us his favour once again. The cooker and fridge-freezer arrived the following week in time for the Christmas parties.

The big day came. The children arrived about two hours early and were patiently waiting outside to be let in. Inside, the volunteers put the finishing touches to the hall and food.

The number of street children that usually came to the club was forty. As I looked out of the upstairs window I counted at least fifty – and there were two hours yet to go! The time went fast and the push of children at the front door increased, as did the noise level.

We had prepared for forty children and welcomed eighty. There were many volunteers that night – including a couple from the embassy. Their help was invaluable as we tried to stretch all the resources to eighty children. There was plenty for everyone, and there was even some left over.

That night, the youngsters feasted like royalty. It was so humbling serving Christmas dinner, Guatemalan-style, to eighty street children. Christmas dinner in Guatemala is *tamales*, small pieces of meat enveloped in a maize dough which are then wrapped in a banana leaf and boiled for hours. These are eaten on their own, washed down with a glass of Coke.

No matter how hungry the children were, they always saved some of their food and put it in their pockets. When I asked them the reason, they said that they had to share it with those who weren't here. We learned so much from the children – at times, more than we actually taught them.

One boy was really having a good time. His name was Leonel, and all the female volunteers would always make a special fuss over him. He had left home and begun living on the streets some years before.

Apparently at some point he had an infection in his foot. The doctor informed me that Leonel had probably left the infection untreated for some time and as a result had contracted elephantiasis. That meant his left leg was about four times larger than normal, and it obviously caused him great pain just to walk. He tried to take part in all the activities and thoroughly enjoyed the evening. His smiling face was a real picture for the photo album. That was the last time we saw Leonel.

Not long after Christmas, two of the volunteers and I were walking into El Hoyo. We saw the children all standing by a wall, looking at the ground. One of the boys rushed over to me, followed by the rest of the group.

'It's Leonel,' they said, 'he's dead!'

I was lost for words – as were the children. One of them grabbed hold of my arm and walked me over to the spot where they had all been standing. Another boy lifted up a filthy piece of cardboard, revealing a pool of blood. It made me shudder and I went into shock; I couldn't believe what I was looking at.

We all sat down nearby. A boy told me how Leonel had been running out of the way of a bus that was passing through the alleyway, when he slipped and fell under the vehicle. The wheels crushed Leonel's head and the pool of blood was where he had died. Some of the children remained standing over the spot, now and again they would lift the piece of cardboard and look. It was af if it was their memorial to Leonel.

I returned home and cried all night. Leonel was the first child I had ever really known who was to die on the streets. During our first year in Guatemala we had known many street children who'd been killed. We even went to some of their funerals. But we didn't know those children the way we knew Leonel.

Every death was hard to deal with. But when you knew the child, that made it a hundred times worse. I must have gone into my own little world for some time as I thought about Leonel and wondered what difference we'd made to his life.

'Is all this work worth anything in the end?' I thought to myself. 'What is the point of all this work if the children just end up dead? And why is God silent when we call out to him every day for a home for the children?'

I told God how I felt – and heard nothing in reply. My pastor came to see me that week and tried to understand what I was feeling.

'Duncan, it's like a race against time with these kids,' he said. 'Sometimes we lose.'

'But I don't want to lose any more!' I shouted. I was angry inside and just needed someone with whom to share my anger.

The following week at the club another boy was causing us problems. Francisco Pablo had broken another window in the church. This time we'd caught him. I phoned the police, who came about one hour after the club closed. We explained the situation. They were totally uninterested and suggested that I just beat him and throw him out on the streets.

I wanted justice and wanted to show the children that we meant what we had said the previous week about breaking another window. I held on to Francisco and decided that Mauricio, one of the volunteers, and I would take him to the local magistrate.

Mauricio thought I was being hard on him and that maybe we should let him go, but I was determined that Francisco should learn a valuable lesson that night. So I put him in our van and drove to zone three, to the magistrates' office. Francisco was protesting loudly, and at one point became violent. We arrived in zone three and went round and round in circles, looking for the magistrates' office.

'So where is it, Mauricio?' I asked. He shrugged his shoulders, indicating his lack of knowledge. Francisco spoke up.

'It's further along this road,' he said. 'You need to turn right there and you will see it on your right.' It seemed funny really – there we were, trying to find the magistrates' office, and only Francisco knew where it was and led us to it! He was arrested and sent to a youth custody centre for four months.

The children returned the following week. From that moment on, we had no more broken windows. Word of Francisco's 'arrest' was the main topic of conversation among the children. They knew we were prepared to act if they continued to damage the property. And I'd learned the hard way in working with young people – you have to get their respect before you can ever become their friend.

Those who tried to become friends with the street children before they gained their respect always had to do things, or provide things, for the children to maintain their friendship. But friendship is something you earn – not something you buy. My daily plea to God at that time was for someone to work alongside me. God provided the funding for a salary for one of the club volunteers.

Back in the UK, Ian Edwards was busy travelling around, telling people about the ministry. Some felt God was calling them to pray. Others believed they were called to give financially. A couple of people felt God was leading them to come and see the work for themselves. It was a hard time for Ian, who was trying to run his own business as well as write letters, travel and speak and cope with the day-by-day administration of a growing charity. His wife Jenni was a great support as was David Stephenson, who works for a firm of accountants.

So funding came our way for a full-time worker to work

with me. He had lived as a street child and was now a completely changed person. But as time went on, he proved to be an unfaithful worker and I had to ask him to leave.

After a false start with a worker who proved unsuitable, God answered our prayers with Mauricio, one of our first volunteers. Mauricio proved to be a faithful man of God who knew this was a calling for which God had prepared him. He was even more excited about his new full-time calling than I was. This really was the beginning of El Castillo, because we were now able to work with the children on a daily basis.

Our regular involvement in their lives paid off, as we were able to help many others. Some children left the streets and went into a government home or a children's home run by an existing childcare agency, or returned to their families. It was thrilling to see some fruit from our labours!

Street children are very good at stealing. They would often come and steal things from my pockets or even from the first-aid bag. The volunteers and I were getting a little wound up about this. So we decided to do something different. We'd been given a large box of New Testaments which we could distribute freely to the children. So we went out that night with our pockets full of Bibles. And just as we'd thought, a couple of street children came to us and tried to steal from our pockets!

One boy reached into my back pocket, pulled out a Bible and then ran off with it down the street. I would have loved to have seen his face when he found out what he actually had in his hand. A short time after, the boy returned smiling.

'So what's this?' he asked me.

'It's a very special letter for you from God,' I replied.

148

He sat down next to me and asked me to read it to him, which I did. Those little Bibles were a great blessing to us and gave us a wonderful opportunity to talk about how much God loved each one of the children.

The work with the girls was increasing. Many were either pregnant or had small children living with them on the streets. Mauricio and I found it hard work trying to build relationships with the girls. Many would look at us as just two more men wanting something from them – even though what we wanted from them was change and a decision to leave the streets.

After much prayer, we felt it right to look for another worker to help us full-time. And this had to be a female worker. One of the volunteers had a sister who, we were told, would be ideal for this ministry and had a heart for street children. We were keen to meet with her and pray together about what God wanted for the ministry.

Two days later, Marta came to see Mauricio and me. After the interview and prayer, we offered her the job and she began to work with us in a full-time capacity. She certainly had the hand of God upon her life – and proved to be a faithful and committed worker for many years.

The ministry was now being effective in helping the children. We made soup once a week and took it to a different group each week. We organised activities during the day for the children and involved ourselves in their world. It was dangerous, rewarding and frustrating. But each day was filled with hope that God would hear our prayer and provide a home so that the children could experience what it was to be part of a Christian family.

Early in 1994 Gary Grant came to visit us. Gary owned a toyshop chain called The Entertainer. He and his wife Cath had kept in touch with us since we left the UK in

1992. After becoming a Christian the year before, Gary wanted to see how he could help.

I believe his first experience of Guatemala was a time that challenged him on many levels. When he returned to England, he and Cath – who'd visited us in Guatemala the previous year – began to speak of their experiences with the street children. Because of his connections with the toy industry and our name, The Toybox Charity, Gary convinced many to help support the ministry. He talked with us about an idea he had of a training centre. Gary was well known in the Amersham area for being a very sharp and shrewd businessman – but whose life had been dramatically revolutionised by Jesus.

The aim was to give street children the opportunity of learning a basic trade or skill. It would be a step up from the existing club. The church had informed us that by the summer they were going to be leaving that site, and we needed to look for other premises to locate the club, so it seemed an ideal opportunity for us to have a full-time centre for the ministry. Jen and I met with Mauricio, Marta and Herbert, another young man who'd been a volunteer with us since the beginning. As we prayed together, we had an overwhelming sense that God was in this – and knew we should push ahead to see if God opened any doors.

Jen and I put together a plan for the new training centre. With Herbert's and Mauricio's help, we looked at how the centre was to operate, what staff would be needed, where would be the best area for it, and when and how the children would be invited to come. The cost of the centre came to £30,000 – over three times the size of our annual budget for running the club and street team. But we trusted that if it was in God's plan, he would provide all that was needed. God's Word reminded us that he would supply all our needs.

We knew God would show us the way. There was also a feeling that he would provide us with someone who had the vision for the centre and who would be prepared to commit themselves to it. God led us to Herbert, a man of God and already one of our trustworthy volunteers. Herbert was a person who we knew listened to God. One of the first evenings we ever met him, he gave us 'a word from God' which he didn't understand and said that when he had finished writing it down he realised it was in English. The note said:

> I brought you here for a vision I put into your heart. Run, my son, slowly but secure. When I called you, you didn't even think I was going to take you so far away. Well, now you are here and I will do much more for you. You have been faithful, I'll be faithful. I love you, let me use you. Prepare yourself because I am leading you on to another thing. Soon you'll have to depart, but deliver the vision to another heart. You thank me all the time – well, let me tell you, thanks, my son. I'll prosper you and your family. Peace to you, says the Lord.

When we began the ministry, we knew God wanted us to launch something that was Guatemalan, not British. I had met many other leaders of Christian ministries in Guatemala. They were all run by Americans or Europeans. After ten or more years of the ministry, no one had been identified as an indigenous leader. I was determined that El Castillo would be a ministry that was run and directed by Guatemalans. Even after hearing that word through Herbert, we knew that the time for us to go had not yet come. But God was telling us to prepare another in our place.

That evening we went to an area called Jocotales, an impoverished, run-down area south of Guatemala City. There was one main road into Jocotales – and one out. The locals were very poor. Many lived in the *baranques*, the unstable slopes on the outskirts. Houses made out of wood and tin, better described as shacks, were cut into the steep ravines which had a 20 to 50 metre drop to the valley floor below. The *baranques* were just places to dump rubbish. Many years of garbage had accumulated in them so that a continual stench emanated from the bottom night and day.

On one of those *baranques* lived hundreds of families – including two boys, Hector and Manuel. We had met Hector on the streets each week and had built a good relationship with him. Through boredom and lack of work, he spent his time sitting in the main square cleaning buses now and again while sniffing glue.

He told us that his father had died a few years earlier and that his mother was very ill. The next time we saw him, he told us his mother had died, and that their family home was in a mess. He didn't know what to do for his little brother, Manuel. We found out that it was soon to be Manuel's birthday, so we asked him if we could see his house and prepare a little party for him. Hector agreed. We planned a cake, party games and food.

On the momentous evening, we arrived in Jocotales and found Hector. He took Herbert, Mauricio, Marta, a volunteer called Maria and me down a steep bank in total darkness. It was hard to see where your feet were going or what was ahead. All we knew was that if we kept to the tall grass on the bank, we'd be safe. Eventually Herbert called out.

'We are here!' he shouted.

It was hard not to trip over the rubbish that seemed to

have been strewn about everywhere. Even though it was dark, we could see that beneath us was a very dark hole – the bottom of the ravine. We crossed over on a plank of wood to his house, which was cut into the side of the ravine. There were no lights. So we lit five or six candles.

'Manuel is not here,' he said, 'I think he might be working.'

As the candles lit up the shack, we could see that the back of the home was the ravine. The sides and front were poorly constructed out of wood, tin and cardboard. It seemed as if the whole thing was about to collapse at any moment. The floor was mud. There was a dog lying down in the corner where a small drawer unit stood next to two beds.

Hector invited us to sit down. It was obvious that the boys had used one corner as a toilet. The dog seemed to use any available space – including the bed! We sat down on the beds, which had no sheets or blankets. A few clothes had been thrown on the beds, and may have been the blankets. We began to sing together and waited for Manuel to return from work.

About an hour later, he arrived and was surprised to see his home lit with candles and full of people singing. As soon as he walked through the door – which was a piece of blue plastic – we all sang 'Happy Birthday' to him. His face was a picture! Shyly, he pushed past us and sat on the corner of his bed. After we'd sung, Maria brought out the birthday cake with some candles on it. Manuel blew them out. We discovered that we didn't have a knife, so Hector went to ask a neighbour.

He returned minutes later with a knife – and his neighbour, who apparently had wanted to know what all the noise was about. She began talking with one of the workers and then left, only to return later with her whole family! She couldn't believe that people would care for these boys and even throw a party for them.

After a few games, Manuel spoke up and said he wanted to say thank you to us for all we had done for his birthday. He then asked us if we could pray for him, as he had been having bad dreams. Apparently his sleep was always disturbed during the night, which, looking around his little shack, wasn't hard to understand.

He said it all started when he first met us and heard about this man called Jesus. One night he woke up and felt someone walking on his bed, but he could see no one there. Then an invisible pair of hands grabbed at his throat, trying to choke him.

He asked Jesus to help him – and immediately the hands left. He didn't understand what was going on in his life. But if God was there, he thought, could he really know this God, just as we said he could? Herbert sat next to him and explained how God showed his love to us and how Manuel could know him and his love from that moment on.

The neighbour found all this very interesting. She asked if we could come back the following week and talk to her family about God! She also wondered if we would consider starting a church in her home. It was all very encouraging. We knew that in order to do that, we would need the help and support of the church we were attending, but when we talked with the pastor of our church about it, he said they were already committed and so couldn't help. We maintained contact with the boys, and began to gather materials to rebuild their home. Six months later the boys left the home – and we only ever saw Hector once again.

Preparations for the training centre were racing ahead. We'd been to view several properties which were either too small or too expensive. Then one evening Jen was reading *El Grafico*, a national newspaper, and found an advert for a five-bedroom house for rent. When we phoned for details, we discovered that the house was only two blocks away from our present home. We went to see it – and fell in love with it instantly. It was £300 a month, and we could occupy it immediately if needed.

We prayed about it, and received news that the Overseas Development Agency (ODA) were interesting in funding half of the project. It seemed like a confirmation later in the same week when the British Embassy called and said they were going to clear out a house and wanted to donate furniture. Did we need any, they asked! We signed a contract with the landlord the following week and took charge of the wonderful big house. It was close to the city centre – yet far enough away – and on the main bus routes.

Herbert came to see us and said he felt that God had confirmed to him something we had discussed the week before, about him working full-time with us. He started a few weeks later as director of the training centre. We had virtually nothing other than a large empty house and three staff, two of whom worked with me on the streets. So we advertised and began to interview prospective staff. Three workers clearly stood out in the first round of interviews and they later formed the training centre teaching staff.

Jen, Herbert and I began to prepare the centre. There was so much to do. In one room I had built benches down one side and thought it would be great if we could find a couple of drawer units. When the furniture arrived from the British Embassy, there were two drawer units that fitted perfectly under the benches. Other furniture included tables, chairs and sofas.

An organisation called Workaid, in England, had shipped out machinery for the centre. A local bank and other businesses heard of what we were doing and donated equipment, clothing and food. The following week we invited the ambassador, business leaders, the church leadership and Gary Grant, who had come over from England, to attend the centre's official opening.

There was a great deal of cleaning to be done. And in the kitchen we found hundreds of cockroaches running about! We bought a few cans of cockroach spray and spent one night spraying around the cooker and the wall units. As we sprayed, literally hundreds of cockroaches came out. Soon the whole wall was black with cockroaches, who were dropping as we continued to spray. It took us another half an hour to spray everywhere – until we were certain they were all dead. Jen and I cleaned them up in the morning, while scraping the thick black grease off the floor with razor blades.

Later that day we went to visit the children on the streets in order to invite some of them to come to the training centre after the weekend. Our philosophy was to look for children who already showed an interest in wanting to leave the streets – those who responded to us when we visited them and were prepared to join in activities. Children who had a desire to change and to learn were invited to the centre, which we called La Torre, or in English 'The Tower', carrying on the theme of castles.

As we arrived at El Hoyo we found that the place was under heavy police guard. The police, assisted by the army, had raided the brothels and bars in El Hoyo that afternoon, and had arrested eleven adults and eleven children. They had found a large quantity of drugs and solvents which were being sold to the street children. The adults were charged with dealing in and using drugs and using the children for prostitution. Apart from the police, El Hoyo was empty that night, and the doors to the brothels were sealed by an official judicial order.

We had brought all our equipment from the church to the centre over the weekend and spent the remaining hours in last-minute preparations and exciting prayer meetings. Little did we know that when we transferred the cooker from the church, we also transferred a whole family of rats with it! They had made a home in the top and bottom of the cooker. We realised that when we tried to heat up the oven and could smell burning. Rats ran around the house for a few days until we were able to catch and kill them all.

La Torre opened on the Monday morning. The group of children we had collected were all keen to explore the centre and tried to rush around to see what was on offer. However, the doors were all locked and the only way in was via the back. There, the children had to leave their clothes and take a shower. They could then choose other clothes before entering the house.

Their day continued with a cooked breakfast, a devotional time – then classes in Spanish, science, maths, woodwork, sewing and computers. I think we aimed our expectations a little high. But slowly the children adapted themselves to the new challenge of learning. It was another dream come true.

8

Miracle Children

Oscar was a street kid literally on the brink of suicide. Burdened with guilt, he decided to punish himself by jumping off a bridge. He had snatched a woman's handbag from her, and now his shoulders carried the weight of bitter regret. He realised he had actually broken one of God's laws.

Determined to carry out his self-imposed sentence, he walked the empty streets of zone one until he came to a big bridge where now and again buses and lorries would pass underneath. He stood on the edge and planned to throw himself off when the next bus or lorry came along. As a vehicle approached, he went to take the final leap – when a mysterious hand grabbed his shoulder and pulled him back on to the pavement.

But when Oscar looked around, there was no one there. The streets were virtually deserted. There was just some occasional traffic and police patrols. Oscar knew that it was God who'd given him another chance. He made a commitment that night not to steal again – and to find out more about God.

Oscar had heard about the Ten Commandments at the training centre. And God had obviously used that to trigger repentance in his heart. This was a miracle in itself. In fact, most street children live by their own group's code of conduct.

The oldest or toughest boys are in charge. The rest follow. The first rule is to share what you have with the rest. Other rules relate to obeying the leader and territory. Some group members may specialise in one activity, like stealing or begging. Often the small children are skilled in those areas. Most sell their bodies for prostitution when they get desperate.

There's also much abuse within the gangs. Younger boys and girls are abused and raped by older ones. Surveys have shown that most street children are sexually active. Most have sexual relations more than once a day.

Territory is important. Some do change groups now and again, but most stay within the same group for many years. The children operate within their territory and lay claim to anything within it.

I've found that some of the children know very little about the rest of the city – only their own little area. Inviting them outside that area for an activity is viewed suspiciously. Some children have refused to join an excursion because of the fear of leaving their patch. Some groups have initiation ceremonies, ranging from daring the would-be gang member to something which involves a high element of risk to a physical or sexual assault.

At one time, a popular trick played by the children was something called *fuegos* which means 'fires'. When a child was asleep their so-called friends got a small piece of newspaper, rolled it into a ball and placed it in the sleeping child's hand or between his legs. The paper was then lit. Then the others would watch until the child woke suddenly, then run away. Not a few children have been literally set alight and disfigured for life with street games such as this.

New gang members always seem withdrawn when we see them for the first time. Early on in the initiation, the new recruit is given a nickname, to be used instead of their real name. The use of nicknames may help the child cope with their new world. Sometimes the nickname is given to emphasise a physical defect, because the child is good at something, or because it reminds the group of an animal or recent film. Names like 'Carrot', 'Cat', 'Rabbit', 'Dirty Face', 'The Wolf' and 'Death' are not uncommon.

Initially the nickname helps us identify them. But as we get to know the children, we prefer to use their real names, if they disclose them. Quite often the youngsters will make up a name for themselves – in fact they very rarely tell you their real name. I've noticed that some children who've left the streets have wanted to change their names after becoming Christians. Their new identity in Jesus means their nickname is something of the past, which they want to leave behind.

There have been so many we have come to know and love over the years. Like Moses or Marleny, they are the miracle children. Coming from homes where they have been abused, raped and tortured, and then having to live on the streets of Guatemala City, it's a miracle they are still alive.

However, not all of them live happily ever after. We do what we can for them. But our path is one of joy and pain, as we watch some of them become miraculously transformed by God's power and love, while others still choose to return to the streets, where they play a constant game with death.

They are real children in real-life situations, with real needs, real fears and real failures. These are some of their stories.

Francisco

On leaving the church building one day, I saw a boy sitting on the side of the road. His hands were squeezing a plastic bag containing glue. I walked over and sat down next to him. We sat there for a while before I said hello and told him my name. No further words were uttered as we both watched the traffic thunder by, now and again fanning the black smoke away from our faces as a bus drove past. Eventually the boy spoke to me.

'My name is Francisco,' he said. Little by little he opened up and then told me his story. Francisco lived with his family in the countryside. He and his father never really got on with each other. His mum would console him every time his father beat him. They were farmers and Francisco had always wanted to travel to Guatemala City. He had heard so many stories of life there.

One day Francisco was invited by his father to go with him to the capital and get some supplies. After sixteen hours on buses, Francisco and his father arrived in Guatemala City. They walked for a while down busy streets, arriving at a large supermarket.

'I'm just going in here to get some supplies,' Francisco's dad said to him, 'wait for me here.' Francisco waited, and waited, and waited. With tears in his eyes he told me how he had waited outside the supermarket for a whole week before he realised that he had been abandoned. Some days, people gave him food. Then a young street boy befriended him and took him to his gang. The boys taught Francisco how to steal, beg, guard and wash cars.

Anything he earned or stole had to be shared with the group. That was one of the basic rules. Francisco also learned how to sniff glue and use drugs.

'They told me it would help,' Francisco said as he got up and pulled out his bag of glue, inhaled and then wandered across to the other side of the street.

I felt a deep sadness watching him destroying his life. It seemed as if he knew no other way and now was so hooked into the street life that he didn't have the strength to get out. I was in pain for him. When I got in the minibus to drive off and looked back in the mirror as Francisco sat inhaling glue, I wished I could force him to do what I knew was right. But I couldn't. I drove away, feeling despair and hopelessness.

Fernando

In a sleepy town called Chicacao in the south of Guatemala, a poor farming family gave birth to a son, Fernando. Life was hard, growing up amid a civil war. And making a living as a farming family meant long hours and enduring hard labour. Just before Fernando was ten years old, his mother died. His father found that he could no longer cope with the children – especially Fernando.

Fernando remembers the various times his father would take him on long journeys into the countryside, and leave him there – in the hope that he wouldn't return home. Fortunately for Fernando, he always found his way back. But each time he was greeted with abuse and violence.

So, at the age of ten, he felt he could make a better life on his own. Leaving behind his father and two little sisters, he headed for the city. There he met up with a group of boys who lived on the streets and shared similar backgrounds.

Very soon Fernando learned to steal and take drugs. His health and state of mind deteriorated as he grew more accustomed to the street culture. Fernando also found that the police, whom he had grown to respect, now became a threat and constant danger to him.

He remembered one night when he and a group of fellow street children were sniffing glue in 6th Avenue. Three uniformed policemen took them by surprise. They began to harass and threaten the children. An officer snatched a bottle of glue from one of the kids and poured it over the children's heads. One boy, Luis, resisted and bore the wrath of the policemen as they kicked him unconscious. He died the following day in hospital.

Because Fernando was a witness to the crime, he reported it to the legal aid office. As charges were brought against the policemen, Fernando began to receive death threats. His life was in danger. He tried to go back to his father. But that attempt failed, and he returned to the streets once again.

Now he begs outside a coffee shop in 8th Avenue, zone one. He's had many threats against his life. Recently he was shot in the leg by a soldier for attempting to steal something from a car. Deep down he knows that, very soon, he too will join his old friend Luis.

The cry of the streets reaches the ears of God each day. Will that desperation also be heard by his Church, which has the power to change the world for these children?

Jorge and Guadalupe

A young homeless family approached me in the streets one day, desperate for help. Every day there are so many demands upon scarce resources. How I wish I could say 'yes' to them all. I'd known Jorge and his partner Guadalupe for about two years. Jorge came to the club one afternoon seeking assistance. He was in a mess, blood pouring from his head.

The week before, he was very excited as he'd been offered a job with a construction company. A new life was now ahead of this nineteen-year-old young man. And he was taking seriously his commitment to his pregnant girlfriend. But crisis had struck.

Apparently he and his work team had just finished a construction job and were returning to the depot. Jorge was standing on the back of the pick-up, guarding and holding equipment in place. The vehicle drove under a low bridge. Jorge had no time to duck. His head collided with the bridge, and he was left lying unconscious in the middle of the road.

When he came to, he found himself back at the depot. And he was told to get to hospital – but return to work the following day. Since the depot was near the club, he came to us first. Mauricio and I placed our hands upon his head to hold it together. When I look back on moments like this, I thank God that even though we had no opportunity for surgical gloves, we suffered no ill effect.

Jorge had a massive hole in his head. He had received quite a severe blow, and it was obvious he was losing a lot of blood, so we rushed him to a private hospital where one of our volunteers worked. I had to stand with Jorge through his operation, as he asked me to hold his hand. Afterwards he just cried. He was in no state to work. So Guadalupe informed the depot of his condition – and they sacked him.

We acted quickly to find accommodation for Jorge and his girlfriend. It was obvious that he was in no state to return to the streets. And Guadalupe was ready to give birth at any moment. One of our volunteers offered a room in his workshop where there was a toilet, sink and bed. We bought them a little stove and some cups, two pans and a couple of plates. They were happy with that. When

I went to visit them after their first child, Jose, was born, they handed me a letter. It said: 'You have helped us forget our pain, hate and bitterness. You have given us joy and happiness so that we don't live with sadness. We have arrived at the point where we see you as older brothers and sisters who know us and give us advice and love from God. Thank you for your kind gifts.'

The team were so encouraged and motivated by this incident to go the extra mile for such children and young people. I still have the letter with me today. It's evidence that God can change even the most desperate of situations.

Miriam

Miriam had left home when she was about fourteen, because her father had regularly raped her over many years. She ended up wandering around the city centre before meeting a group of girls about her age in a park.

Slowly a relationship developed between Miriam and the girls, because she was sleeping just yards away from the group. She soon realised that survival meant having to beg or steal in order to live one more day. The other girls had another way of making money – prostitution. And it wasn't long before Miriam was selling her body to total strangers. She put up with the indignity of it all, because her life depended on it.

The street team had regular contact with the group and so came to know Miriam. She was a shy girl but always full of life. Marta, one of our street team, had asked Miriam if she could make contact with her family to see if there was any possibility of letting them know that Miriam was alive. Miriam agreed. But she asked that her whereabouts be kept secret.

Marta found the family home in the middle of a very

poor neighbourhood. She talked for a couple of hours with Miriam's mother. The woman explained that her husband had left home soon after Miriam, and that she would like Miriam to come back home.

Miriam couldn't believe the news of her father's flight from the home. But she agreed to allow her mother to make contact with her. The following week, Marta brought Miriam's mother to 19th Street, where Miriam was living. The two women had an emotional reunion, but Miriam was not ready to return home at first.

As the weeks went by, both Marta and Miriam's mother pleaded with Miriam to return home each time they saw her. And it looked as though Miriam's heart was softening. Eventually she told Marta that she would return home the following day. She just needed time to collect her things – stored in hiding holes around the centre – and say goodbye to her friends. They agreed to meet around 9.00 a.m. the next day at a local bridge.

Marta was quite ill that night and was unable to go to work the following day. She didn't call into the office to arrange for someone else to meet with Miriam, who must have waited on the bridge for some time for Marta to arrive.

When Marta returned to work the following day she went to find Miriam and was shocked to find out that, that night, Miriam had been attacked by a group of men with machetes. Police found pieces of her body scattered around the park. The news hit Marta with full force. She still carries the guilt with her today.

Americo

Late one evening, Marta was walking back from Concordia Park to where the minibus was parked. A group of older street children – most of them unknown to us – stood in her way. One of the boys grabbed Marta's arm and began to threaten her and the team.

Then he lit a cigarette, inhaled deeply, took it from his mouth and held it over her arm. As if from nowhere, seventeen-year-old Americo appeared, accompanied by some other street children.

He jumped on the boy who was seeking to burn a hole in Marta's arm. Then he and his gang chased her aggressors away. Marta and the team were waiting to see what the boy was going to do before reacting, but were astonished by the speed of Americo's defence.

'Americo returned like some battle-worn hero,' said Marta. 'Sweating profusely and heart pounding, he asked if I was all right. I was still coming to terms with what had happened. Americo was always a very respectful young man. He had a great smile and would always be looking around us for danger whenever we were on the streets.'

Marta asked him why he had done such a brave thing.

'I like you because you don't just talk about love,' he replied.

She sat down with him on the crumbling steps of the Burger King restaurant and told him about God's love. He said he would think about it, and would tell her what he thought the next time he saw her. But we never saw him again. The following week, Americo was shot dead outside a shop by a security guard who said he was stealing.

Alex

Alex's mother had given birth to him on her thirteenth birthday. She'd run away from El Salvador at the age of twelve. When her money ran out, and with nowhere else to live, she set up home on the streets of Guatemala City.

Born into destitution, life had never been easy for Alex. With no father and his mother very young and inexperienced, Alex spent more and more time alone on the streets or with other street children. He became more accustomed to the sub-culture of street life. And that resulted in frequent visits to Guatemala's notorious prisons.

Life in the gang had its ups and downs. Alex slept near to the central bus station. It was there that he met a woman who told him about how God had changed her life – and how God could do the same for him.

Each day she would return and tell him more about the plans God had for his life. Two weeks later Alex became a Christian. He left the streets. But his old mates tried to contact him and entice him back. He found the desire to return very strong, but always resisted. He is now married and attends a church in Guatemala City.

My dream was to employ a small team of people who would work specifically with those like Alex, who were at high risk of becoming street children. That team would also cope with any follow-up work generated by contact made with the street children and their families. Resources were few to turn this dream into reality. But I knew that when the time was right, God would supply all that was needed.

Michael

Imagine what it would be like to be born in one country, then grow up in another, and then have to return to your native land – only to end up living out on the streets. Michael still lives there, in Concordia Park. His ruddy face hides a deep inner sadness and frustration at being stranded in a country he knows little about – and cares even less to live in.

When Michael was two, his mother and father had travelled to California where they'd both been offered work. Their new life was exciting. They sought to deny the huge differences there were between them. As Michael grew, he began to study in a school and had a promising future ahead of him.

His parents would often argue. He would run and hide in the garden to avoid conflict. But the day came when his dad told him that he and his mum were getting divorced. Michael's dad was going to return to Guatemala and Michael had to come too, as his mum wanted to begin a new life on her own.

Returning to Guatemala was a big culture shock. Michael and his dad managed to move in with relatives, and his dad started to look for work. After a few months, Michael's dad told him that he wanted to get married. But there was a snag. His wife-to-be would only marry him 'uncluttered' by children. In no uncertain terms, Michael was told to leave home. He was only eight years old.

In Guatemala, childhood is a pleasurable experience for the few – and a luxury for the many. That's particularly so for the children with whom I work. Their recollections of what we would know as childhood are so painful that they're locked deep within the child's memory and surface only when the child feels secure enough to lower his or her defences.

The term 'childhood' describes a very precious and necessary time of development that parents and society have a duty to safeguard and protect. It is in childhood that the individual can explore the world in relative safety and can be kept from experiencing things that would damage their ability to grow into maturity.

To watch a seventeen-year-old boy sit down and play with two toy cars like a six-year-old made me wonder why this experience was new for him. The car noises that came out of his mouth, as he screamed the cars along the floor, were noises that you would normally hear coming from an infant. We have found that the street children need to be given the opportunity of enjoying childhood – even though it may be many years later.

Nelson

Nelson and his younger brother lived in the countryside. He told me he'd been constantly abused by both his mother and his father. But when his brother was five, his parents started to abuse him instead of Nelson. After a year of watching his brother suffering, Nelson decided to act.

Early one morning Nelson left home with his young brother and hitched a ride to Guatemala City. Not knowing anything about urban life, the two boys wandered around the capital for hours. Eventually, hungry and thirsty, they found a market and went in to beg for food, only to find that people weren't very generous.

The two boys were holding hands, pushing through the crowds, and at one point got separated. Nelson began searching for his little brother but couldn't find him. As the hours passed, Nelson became more anxious about his brother and continued searching for him, but in vain. He told me he went back to the market to look for him. But he's never seen him since.

Nelson is such a quiet boy. One wonders why he is on the streets at all. I believe that he continues to punish himself for what happened to his brother by living in that environment.

Marleny

Marleny has experienced the worst that life can throw at you. But she is able to say that it's because of Jesus that today she is a changed woman. Marleny came off the streets in September 1996 at the age of fifteen and, together with a small group of her friends, was offered a place in the training centre. A year later I talked with Marleny about her life and how it was that she had changed so much. She explained it all in a letter:

I was born on Christmas Eve. When I was five, my mother gave me to a lady because she did not want me any more. The lady made me beg on the streets for money. And when I was nine, I was forced to have sex with many men. If I refused I would be burned with lighted cigarettes. I have many scars now because of this.

Then I was given away to another family, who would beat me all the time. The man in the family raped me. As a result of this, I got pregnant. When the baby was born, they took it off me and I ran away to live on the streets. Because of these experiences I grew up with a hatred in my heart against all men who tried to become 'my friend'. I am ashamed to say that I became a lesbian, because women aren't as bad as men and my girlfriend made me feel safe and secure.

That was two years ago, before I met a group of Christians who told me about God and gave me somewhere to live. I knew I needed to change. I didn't want to keep living like that. I was tired and – most of all – I was hurting God. I want to change for him. I left that girl to live for Jesus. Now I have a future, I am studying and want to be a professional. I would like, one day, to get married and give my life for God's service.

Rolando

Rolando and his friends were sleeping when the van pulled up in front of them. An armed man got out and started shouting at the boys. Rolando sat up. The man grabbed him and pulled him into the van. As they drove away, the man told Rolando how he and his friends were sick and tired of the street children, and that Rolando was about to die.

The previous Sunday, Herbert, the director of the project in Guatemala, had taken Rolando to church with him. After the service Rolando had asked for prayer. A couple of people prayed for him, then gave him a Christian leaflet.

During his death ride in the van, Rolando remembered the leaflet and pulled it out of his pocket. He was crying and thinking about how many more minutes he had before he would die. As he looked at the literature, Rolando began to pray. He asked God to keep him safe.

The man snatched the booklet from him and handed it to the driver. Within minutes the van turned around. They dropped Rolando back where they'd picked him up. God had heard his call.

Rolando is still on the streets of Guatemala.

Moses

I've met many children through my work, but none quite like Moses. He was always a very tough street boy. And he wasn't afraid to use violence to get what he wanted and maintain his position within the group. He grew up in the coastal area of Guatemala. With darker skin than most, he was given the nickname Negro, which means 'the black one'.

Moses ran away from home at eight years of age. He doesn't remember who his father was – his mother never talked about him. She used to beat Moses, and he remembers that the physical violence got worse as he grew up. If Moses was late from school or didn't do his chores on time or to the standard she expected, she would beat him.

Moses would be struck with sticks and rods. Sometimes he would have his hands tied together and would then be tied up from a beam in the house so that his feet dangled above the floor. Often he would be stripped naked and his mother would throw cold water over him and give him electric shocks or burn his skin with cigarettes. After a few years of such torture, Moses ran away from home and found himself in Guatemala City.

Now Moses is wise to everything and is totally immersed in the street culture. He has been in and out of our boys' home as well as other institutions and youth custody centres. I believe what God has begun in his life he will bring to completion one day. So we trust him into God's hands.

The national police arrested Moses one evening and drove him out of Guatemala City. Once at a suitable spot, the police car stopped and the officers pulled Moses out. They put a gun to his head and began to tell him they were being paid to clean up the streets of scum like him.

Just then, a car came round the corner and the headlights shone directly on the policemen. They put their guns away and waved at the motorist to keep driving. The driver clearly thought they were telling him to slow down and stop, which he did. Seeing an opportunity before him, Moses rolled over and fell down a steep embankment.

He escaped and lived to tell the tale. Moses is now trying again to leave the streets through the Toybox project.

Jose

Mauricio and I were invited to a church in the south of Guatemala City to speak about the street children ministry. Just before we about to speak, there was a power cut. Everyone left the church building and walked out into the street where there was still some light.

As we stood around in the church car park I noticed a young man staggering up the road in our direction. Some of the church members moved back towards the building when the young man walked into the car park, shouting and swearing. Mauricio and I were standing at the front of the car park and so were first in line to be shouted at.

'So what are you looking at?' the young man shouted at me. I didn't have a response – at least not a nice Christian one – so I said a quick prayer to God.

As I did so, with the young man looking into my face, I felt God telling me that he was called Jose. The reason he was living like that was because when he was young he was left alone, abandoned, and had been drinking himself into the ground and living on the streets.

'What are you looking at?' he shouted once again.

'I see a man who needs God,' I replied. 'Tell me your name.' When he said his name was Jose, I knew then that I'd just heard God speak to me and needed to tell him the rest.

'Well, Jose,' I continued, 'God says that he knows why you are living like this on the streets and drinking all day and all night – because when you were young you were abandoned and you have been angry ever since.' He was silent. Then he spoke up.

'So how do you know all this?' he said.

I explained to him that God loved him and wanted a relationship with him. All he needed to do was to ask for forgiveness for something God already knew about and had just revealed to him, and he would be forgiven. Jose did. And as he said he wanted to come and find out more, the electricity came back on. We invited him to come with us into church. I believe his life started to change that night. We left him in the care of that local church.

Chiqui

Chiqui is a pretty girl who looks a lot younger than seventeen. I have known her since she was twelve, when she was living with a group of street girls in 18th Street. Many of the girls would rent rooms in cheap hotels from time to time, especially when the business of prostitution demanded it.

Chiqui never told us why she ran away from home. But she was always bubbly and full of life. Her bright eyes always shone out, and her smile was ever-present, regardless of what situation or circumstances she was in. I found it hard to understand why anyone would want to abuse such a beautiful girl.

As Chiqui grew up on the streets, her appearance deteriorated dramatically. Her clothes were torn and dirty, where once they had always been clean and tidy. Her hair was rarely combed and her nails were now long and black. But the smile was still there – even though you could tell it was more of a strain to show it.

What most upset me about Chiqui was the way her

mind worsened the more she took drugs. It became harder to have a conversation with her, as her concentration was very limited.

Every Tuesday the street team would visit the girls in 18th Street. They would take them some soup, organise activities and encourage them to join in a time of worship. The girls would always be waiting for the team to arrive. Many refused to 'work' while we were with them.

One evening the girls were waiting for the team to arrive when the bus the workers were travelling in broke down. The next day one of the workers tried to explain to the girls why they hadn't come the night before.

'But we were waiting for you,' said one of the girls. The team felt discouraged that they had let the girls down. But Chiqui had the final say.

'Well, even though you didn't come, we still had church,' she said, 'and I preached for you!'

The policeman

There have been many experiences of God turning up at the right time and getting me and the team out of a hole. The story of the policeman was just one such occasion.

We were wandering around the bus terminal. It was about 10.00 p.m. and most of the market stalls were closed down for the night. But there were still plenty of people on the streets. The bus terminal is a busy place and a good spot to look for new groups of children. That's where some would spend their first night on the streets.

I spotted two little girls sitting down by the side of the road. Their clothes were shabby and they were obviously in need of a good bath and a hot meal. The team and I approached the girls. I sat down next to them, said hello, and asked them their names. Shyly, they looked at each other and then down at their feet.

Just then a woman appeared next to me and asked what I was doing. I stood up and explained what we were seeking to do on the streets and that I wanted to find out if these girls needed help.

With anger in her voice, the woman told me that they were her daughters and that they were just waiting for her husband to come and then were going home – what business was it of mine, anyway? As she said that, a tall, well-built man stood next to her. He wanted to know what was going on. A small crowd of people was now gathering.

Usually when we begin to work with the children on the streets, a small crowd of people forms to watch what we do and see how the children respond. Most times such on-lookers don't bother us and are not a distraction. But in situations like this one, a crowd is an unwelcome thing.

'What are you doing, talking to my daughters?' said the man. Most Guatemalans are rather suspicious of foreigners talking to children.

'I am with a small team of people who work with street children,' I said. 'And part of our job is to find children who've recently arrived on the streets. We wish to befriend them so we can help them.'

The man became very angry and began to threaten us. 'I am a policeman,' he said, 'and I have a gun. And I don't take kindly to my daughters being referred to as street children.'

He obviously wanted to teach us a lesson! I tried to help him see we were just attempting to do our job. He said he was trying to do his as well – as a father and as a policeman.

'But we work for the Lord Jesus Christ!' one of our workers shouted out. I expected the man to do exactly what he had threatened. Instead, he began to cry.

'I used to know Jesus Christ,' he said through his tears. 'Can you please tell me how I can know him again?' The situation was totally turned around with the mention of the name of Jesus.

Daniel and Carolina

We had been working with the children of Concordia Park for about an hour when one of the workers came to me to ask for my help. An older street boy had been stabbed in the back and was obviously in some pain. I applied a very strong surgical tape to his wound which would act as a temporary stitch, aided by two visitors from England, Nick and Kate Austin.

When I returned to where the street team were, I heard screams. A young girl came running over to me. She was clutching a small boy, and in her face I could see fear.

'Please help me, Duncan,' she said, and without taking a breath continued, 'someone's trying to steal my son!' I looked at her, then at her little boy who must have been about two years of age.

'Why is someone trying to steal your son?' I asked, feeling sure that I had misinterpreted what she had said to me.

'That lady over there tried to steal Danny. She has tried before – but this time she nearly took him from me.'

I asked Mauricio to help while another member of the team took Carolina and Daniel to sit in the safety of the minibus. As we approached the woman Carolina had said was trying to steal her son, she smiled. In a roundabout way, I tried to ask why she had shown an interest in Daniel. The lady explained that she too had lost a son, and was looking for a replacement.

'If I can't have him back,' she said, 'I'll steal another one!'

She was obviously in pain at the loss of her young son. But this was no way to make things right!

Our concern for that moment was Carolina and Daniel. So we walked back to the minibus and talked with Carolina about what her options were. She had calmed down a little and was able to talk, with little Danny asleep on her lap.

She could either go back to the streets where she and Daniel had been living for some time, or come with us. The words that I had wanted to say for so many years came quickly out of my mouth.

'Well, why not come and live in our home?' We explained about the boys' home and that it would be a short-term option until more suitable accommodation could be found.

Carolina agreed. So we drove her and Daniel up to the boys' home. The next morning I went up to the home to see how they were doing. Only Daniel was awake, and was wearing a very soiled nappy and a t-shirt. I got him showered and dressed. But he didn't say a word.

When he was clean, he said, 'Drink'. So I took him to the kitchen and found him a glass of milk and something to eat. He sat on my knee and looked up into my eyes. He didn't smile but said the word 'Daddy'. Then quickly he followed that with the word 'belt'.

For the first few weeks he could only say 'drink', 'food', and 'Daddy-belt'. He could not say 'Daddy' without saying the word 'belt'. On the right-hand side of his face was an obvious mark of abuse. You could very clearly see that someone had bitten him on the cheek, and not just lightly either – this was a hard bite which had left a ring of teeth marks. There were other marks on his body to confirm the regular use of the word 'belt'.

Daniel and Carolina never went back to the streets and now live in the girls' home. Daniel is struggling with the little affection and care he receives from Carolina and is demonstrating violent tendencies.

Moses and Paula

It was the turn of the girls from 19th Street to come to The Tower. They came with a plea of help for two little children they had found abandoned in the streets. Moses and Paula were only two and three years old, and were asleep under the bridge. The street team went out to find them.

They couldn't see the infants immediately, but heard that they were being looked after by a lady at one of the notorious hotels in 18th Street. The previous day police had arrested a prostitute in 19th Street for stealing. She had two young children with her. But still the police arrested her – and left the two children, two and three years of age, on the streets!

Not surprisingly, the toddlers were very distraught. The street team brought them back to the training centre where they had a shower, changed their clothes and enjoyed a hot meal. After a few days the mother was released from prison and came to collect her children, taking them back to live on the streets while she sold herself in prostitution. They still live on the streets today.

Pablo

Pablo left home because he'd suffered many years of abuse. He and his younger brother would always fight. Pablo would always get the blame – and the punishment.

One day he and his brother were arguing, and in a moment of rage Pablo killed his younger brother.

Pablo was about eleven when he fled from home. Filled with anger and hatred, he ran away to Guatemala City. He soon found out there were others like him, who had also run away from home and were now living on the streets. He was invited to join a group of children who lived in one of the central parks. The group he became friends with are nearly all dead now.

Little Pablo only acted out what he saw happening all around him – people not facing up to conflict but rather responding with violence. In troubled homes and out on the street, children learn that's the only option. So very often they take that route. This is a generation facing death well before their time. They should not have to deal with that.

Sadly, Pablo continues to live on the streets. He and his gang were forcibly removed from the park which had been their home for many years to make room for a new city centre car park.

9

Passing on the Torch

How do you turn a square concrete building into an enchanted palace? Whatever the formula is, it seemed we had stumbled upon it. The Tower opened each day to about twelve children. It was great to see them arrive in the minibus. They were all excited at the prospect of a day away from the streets.

We had arranged the house so that there was a central workshop as you entered the building, with two class-rooms and a kitchen. To the rear of the ground floor was a bathroom where the children would shower and change their clothes.

On the second floor was a large lounge with seats and a TV. Off that room were an office, a medical examination room and two bedrooms, one of which Jen and I used. On the flat roof the owners had constructed two rooms. One was used as a store, and the other was home to our armed guard and his family.

Most of the children who came thought that The Tower would be a good skive and a place where they could eat, shower and sleep. We had to convince them that if they wanted to come off the streets and make something of their lives, then they would have to put much effort into it. It was a difficult breaking-in period.

That proved to be another point of conflict as the children were keen to run the centre. For a few weeks they refused to come, saying that it was too strict. We relaxed the programme to allow them to do some of the things they wanted to do, like extra sports activities, and to rest more. And we needed to help them see the importance of learning a trade or skill.

The children began to return and put much effort into making The Tower work. The staff planned more recreation time for them. They took them to a nearby park where they could run around and enjoy some team sports, which also helps the detoxification process.

Exercise does in fact help them tremendously. After something to eat and drink the children can run around for an hour before they need to rest. Getting fresh air into their lungs gives them a healthier look. The children themselves tell us that they feel better after taking part in some sport rather than sniffing glue.

We don't have an official health survey or document to explain the process. But we know that it helps! Jen believes that it's not the sport that detoxifies them, but rather the fact that while they're playing they're not taking drugs.

The Tower was becoming established, and we realised more and more that the time was coming for us to leave the work. Since receiving a prophecy when we first started the Castillo ministry, we had felt that God was preparing us to return to the UK. And as the months went by, we believe God confirmed that was his will and timing.

We'd prayed for a local team to take over the project and for confirmation that God had something for us to do when we returned that would benefit the work among the street children. We knew we could never walk away from all that God had done through us and in us, and forget the children. Whatever was ahead of us had to be key in the future development of the work to help the street children we had adopted into our hearts in Guatemala.

A few months after the The Tower opened Jenni and Katelyn made the first move back to the UK. I'd planned to foliow them a few weeks later. I needed more time to spend with the new staff at the centre. The street team were working very well and were making contact with about a hundred children each week.

We still needed reassurance that God was with us. On one particular difficult day Jen and Katelyn had to make a trip across the city centre, so they took the minibus. Jen was feeling tired and vulnerable. As they drove through zone one, across the bridge where many street children hang around during the day, Jen felt sad at all she could see around her. She began to cry. Saying nothing to Katelyn, who was sitting in the front passenger seat, she called out to God in her mind.

'God, I just need to know that you are there,' she prayed. Just then, Katelyn pointed out of the window.

'Look, mummy – I can see angels! They're watching over us!' she exclaimed. Jen felt intensely comforted, knowing that God was in control of the situation, and that he would send his angels to look after me when she and Katelyn returned to Britain.

It was an emotional farewell at Guatemala City airport the following week. Many people from our church had turned up, as well as all the staff and volunteers from the ministry.

We both knew this would be a hard time for us. But we also knew that we had to trust God's leading and that he knew best how to help the children. As I watched the plane take off, I decided the best way to cope was to keep busy and try to invest as much time as I could with the street children before I left a few weeks later, at the end of November.

Back in the UK, Ian Edwards was struggling to cope with the increased interest in our work. He was clearly under a lot of pressure. His full-time job was highly demanding, which often meant him returning home very late. Then he would begin to answer letters for the charity, all by hand, and try to give up some of his weekends to travel to churches and interest groups to inform them about the Toybox ministry.

It was clear that he couldn't carry on living like that. We needed someone in the UK who'd experienced the ministry and could effectively communicate how God was at work in the lives of the children and staff. It became very clear that we could fit this position. But if we returned, where would we live? How would we live? What did God want us to do next?

We committed all these uncertainties to God in prayer, and sought answers to our questions. About that time I met with a Guatemala Christian and talked to him about handing over the ministry to local people. His response shocked me. I had explained to him that we were praying about returning to the UK. Since the first day God had spoken to us about the ministry, we had a strong sense that he was saying we needed to put it in the hands of local people. That had been confirmed by the prophecy we received.

'But who is going to come from England and run the ministry?' was his question. I explained again that we felt God wanted the ministry to be run by nationals.

'But you can't leave it in the hands of Guatemalans,' he said. 'They need someone to lead them or else they will just run off with the money.' Here was a Guatemalan telling me not to trust Guatemalans, which was slightly bizarre. But I decided to listen to what he said, and then do what we knew God wanted anyway.

Herbert, twenty-four, and Mauricio, twenty-two, were two young men God had clearly called to take a lead in the charity's work. After a year in the ministry it was obvious that their hearts were being changed and that they were being set apart for leadership. They were now coming to me with ideas and plans. Before, it had been the other way around. God was filling them with his Spirit and giving them a wisdom beyond their years.

God was showing us we could trust the Guatemalan ministry into his hands and that it was his responsibility to provide the workers for the harvest field. It was our responsibility to trust and pray; and what a team of dedicated people God raised up for us to pass on the baton.

However, it was not all plain sailing. There have been setbacks, with staff who have betrayed our trust and have either stolen from us or used their position in the ministry to meet their own needs.

Back in the UK, Gary and Cath Grant had invited us to consider moving into their annexe and living with them. Many questions were still left unanswered. But the way things started to come together was a sign to us that God was moving us on from Guatemala to something new in England.

It would be so difficult to leave. But we had to trust that our going would benefit the ministry more in the long term than we could see in the present. So we began to make plans.

There was much to do as we planned the work ahead and how the staff could run projects to help the street children. I led a couple of training days explaining to the new staff the vision of El Castillo, how it all began and what our objectives were for the coming year. I thought it important that each member of staff felt they could own the vision and could share in the process of demonstrating

God's love to the street children in practical ways – not just preaching at them and asking them to say a prayer of commitment.

Our frustration was always that of not having a home for the children. Those children who had started a process in the training centre were doing well. But we had nowhere permanent to offer them – apart from referring them to two other existing agencies that worked with the street children. The organisation Jen and I had worked for was the easiest to take the children to – especially younger boys, since younger boys were considered a more teachable group than older boys. We struggled with placing a couple of girls in homes.

A Christian family made contact with us and wanted to know if we had thought about asking for adoptive parents for the children. However, when they visited the centre and met some of the children, they decided it would never be possible. I think they had in mind very small children who just needed a cuddle and everything would be all right. When they met fourteen- and sixteen-year-olds who were very streetwise – and whose language and appearance would, they said, destroy their credibility in church – they confirmed that the only option was to build homes for them. One particularly painful experience showed us the importance of such shelter and security – and the need to get it right.

We were trying to find a home for sixteen-year-old Sandra, who had just given birth to a little girl. Sandra had confidence in us because Jen had spent much time with her. She trusted us when we suggested that, since we didn't have a home for street girls, she allow us to contact other agencies to see if a suitable place could be found.

A few days later we received a call from an evangelical group that had been established a few years previously.

The organisation had been given permission to evangelise street children, and were given land and homes by the Guatemalan government.

We'd heard very little of this group. But we were impressed during our first visit to one of the homes just outside Guatemala City centre. The home was run by the director and his wife, and there were various units for the girls to live in. It all seemed like a dream for Sandra. So we arranged for her to visit the centre the following day.

As two of our workers arrived with Sandra and her baby, they were shown around. They could see that Sandra was falling in love with the place. She didn't need to be convinced that this would be the right step for herself and her newborn baby. So the workers left Sandra and her baby there, and returned with the good news that they'd now found a home. We were all very encouraged.

After a few days we phoned the centre to find out how Sandra and the baby were getting on. We were given no news and were asked to phone in a few days – which we did. When we called, we were told that Sandra was no longer at the home but had run away.

We had become used to such disappointments. Tragically, it was becoming all too easy to hear the news of yet another child who had rejected the love you had given them and the plans you thought best for their life. Sandra's story was to prove slightly different from the norm.

Later that evening our workers found Sandra on the streets. She was in a mess. She had obviously been taking drugs again. Her hair was unkempt, she screamed at the team and was in an emotionally unstable state. As the workers began to get alongside her, she poured out her hurt.

The staff noticed that she was alone on the street. Immediately they feared for the safety of her baby. We were told Sandra had left the baby at the centre but was planning to return there and collect her. But Sandra never returned. Later we understood why.

When our staff left Sandra at the home, she was shown to a room and told that was where she could sleep. Her baby was taken from her so that she could be examined. The staff at the centre thought it best to keep Sandra at a distance from her child. Throughout the day Sandra would ask to see her child, but was denied access.

After a few days, Sandra found out that the centre's director and his wife had recently lost a little baby girl. Apparently the little girl who'd died had shared the same name as that of Sandra's baby. The couple kept Sandra's child at their house, and in the same room as the child who had died – with the same clothes and same toys. They'd simply replaced their own lost child with Sandra's baby.

One morning Sandra was allowed to see her baby, but not to hold her. The couple had taken her child to be their own and made it very clear that Sandra could have access to her only at certain times in the week. The sight of her baby in someone else's arms was too much for Sandra, who felt that she had been robbed. She returned to her room, gathered up her few possessions and ran away from the centre. Sandra was back to square one, living out a daily near-death experience on the streets of Guatemala City.

We were very angry. We phoned the centre. The director told us that since Sandra had left the centre, they had registered the baby as abandoned. Then they began proceedings to adopt the baby for themselves. They thought that would be best for the infant, as Sandra wouldn't be able to cope with her on the streets and that she would only die there anyway!

It was outrageous. But legally we were powerless to do anything about it. The facts were plain. Sandra had left the home without her child. So the baby had been registered as abandoned. We were advised that we had a nil chance of getting Sandra's baby back through the courts, since she had 'abandoned' her in the home. We didn't have a leg to stand on nor a lawyer to fight the case – nor would Sandra want to go through the whole ordeal.

We cried out to God for justice. But none came. Sandra told the other girls what had happened. We ended up as the bad guys because we'd taken Sandra to the centre and couldn't get her baby back. The staff were feeling very alone and wondered why all this was happening. When would God give us the homes we had asked him for so long ago?

I could reason with them and say that it was all in God's time. But that didn't make any sense. God is King of the universe and owns all things. It wouldn't take him long to sort out a couple of homes for us so we could offer the children an alternative place to stay. We sat with Sandra. We cried with her. We shouted out to God together. And we waited for his time to come.

Sandra was obviously deeply upset. But in talking through the issues with her, she admitted that her baby would now have a better future with this family, so she could feel that she had made the best decision as a mother. We had to realise, too, that there are certain things the system throws at you in which you can only pray and leave the matter in the hands of God.

Furthermore, that incident proved to us all how important it is for Christians to become actively involved in the projects they support. We are called by God to be responsible stewards of our money. That means making sure that what you give really is used for the purposes publicised, and that – so far as you know – the groups you are supporting aren't undertaking unorthodox practices like taking babies from single mothers.

Particularly for groups of churches in a certain area, it's always worth funding a trip for a representative to go and visit the project and talk with the staff about how effective the ministry really is before committing money to a seemingly bona fide cause.

When I returned from Guatemala in December 1994 and began to travel to many different places around the UK, I was grateful for the opportunity to speak in quite a number of churches. However, I have been saddened by those who have taken a short-term and apparently superficial interest in the street children. Such actions can put you in the dangerous position of simply easing your conscience rather than entering into the world of the poor and suffering to the extent that it challenges your lifestyle.

By contrast it is a delight to work with local churches that support the charity on a consistent basis and welcome regular feedback of how the money given is used. They can also pray into the situation until they see God's Kingdom come in power, and remain faithful to that ministry until God clearly calls them into another area.

That way the regular news will encourage them to pray and give praise to God. They will see that God hears and answers prayer. And they will be able to enter into the world of the chosen ministry which will challenge them into a deeper involvement into the lives of real people rather than supporting a faceless crowd of poor people who need some money.

When it came time for me to return to England, I was torn. Here in the lovely country of Guatemala I was leaving behind my friends – and the children still out on the streets. The hardest part was feeling that Jen and I had achieved so little during the last two-and-a-half years. The children were still there on the streets. We had given them hope. But we were still waiting on God to give us a home for them. And until that came, we would continue to cry out to him for justice and mercy.

During my last hectic week in Guatemala I made time to visit the various groups of street children and explain to them that I was leaving. I had told them before, but now they seemed to take in the reality of my departure. Most of the children reacted with anger, shouting at me and saying that I was just like all the rest who came into their lives and then left them.

I tried to explain that it was best for me to return to the UK because I needed to tell people about the children living on the streets and pray for the money needed to build a couple of children's homes. I knew it was best for them in the long term and that God wanted a Guatemalan ministry to street children – not an imported British one.

I knew that what I was leaving behind was something far better than just me alone. I took some comfort in reflecting how it must have been hard for Jesus to say goodbye to his disciples and return to heaven. But he knew that what was to come would be far better. I had to trust that my leaving behind the street children would pave the way for something better for them, too.

I sat down with a group of children in El Hoyo the night before I left. I talked about their lives and how I was trusting them to God and the local workers. They knew that when I returned I wanted to see them off the streets. We chatted together for what seemed like hours, sitting in the back of a burnt-out lorry.

Doctor Henry climbed in the lorry and sat down in front of me. We'd given Henry his new nickname because he was always willing to give a hand with the first-aid kit, he always smiled when we called him Doctor.

He'd been stealing and came to show the other children a pile of computer games he had taken from a market stall when the stall holder's attention was distracted by a fight in the streets. I expect the fight was performed by the other children! The children played with the games until the batteries ran out, then discarded them in the corner of the lorry. They had no further value to them and so were worthless.

I knew the children weren't happy about me leaving. But it didn't seem to matter that night, as I wasn't leaving till the morning. The important thing to the children was that moment. Tomorrow was another day – and they might not even be alive then.

The children have so little in many ways. Yet I have learned so much from them. They have learned that precious gift of enjoying the moment. They absorb it for what that moment can offer, for nothing else, no plans of tomorrow, no worries about what another day will bring, just enjoying being together, talking and enjoying each other's company.

Some of the boys lay down on the floor of the lorry and looked up at the stars. As I gazed up to the heavens, it was truly a wonderful sight.

'So what airline are you going with and what time is your plane leaving tomorrow?' one of the boys asked me.

'American Airlines, and I'll be leaving at 11.00 a.m.,' I replied. 'Why do you want to know? Are you coming to see me off, then?'

'No,' he said, 'I just want to know because at 11.00 a.m. we will all look up into the sky at your plane and then we will be sad.'

The impact of his response hit me hard. How could I leave these children, I asked myself. Would it really all work out by leaving the ministry in the hands of local people? It was a special and emotional goodbye. The next day I left Guatemala City with such a heavy heart.

Yet I still feel part of those children – more so than part of the British culture. I can easily understand them, and the reasons why they think the way they do. I don't have to struggle to enter into their world. I can remember how I felt, many years ago, being thrown out of my own home – and wishing that someone had come into my life and said, 'Here, take my hand.'

I could identify with their pain and displacement. I could understand so much more because, in part, I had been there. I knew a little of how it feels to be lonely in a crowd of people – hungry, homeless and unwanted. God had brought me a long way and now I was being used to help others take their next step from loneliness to belonging, from inner bondage to the joy of release. And now I was delegating the hands-on part of the work to an indigenous team, rather than an imported outsider.

Some of the staff had come to see me off. The rest were working at the training centre. But I was most encouraged that two street children had come to say goodbye as well. As the plane took off, we flew right over El Hoyo at 11.05 a.m. – and I knew the children would be looking up and feeling sad. I looked out of the window as tears welled up in my eyes and cried for them. It was all right for me. I could get on a plane and leave.

On my return to the UK I experienced a whole range of emotions. There was joy at seeing Jen and Katelyn waiting for me at other side of customs. But we knew a part of us would always remain behind in Guatemala with the children.

Settling back into life in Amersham had its own challenges. We praised God for the Grants, the wonderful family who had invited us to share their house just outside the town. The fact that it was a large house in spacious grounds made the transition harder from impoverished Guatemala to comfortable Britain. But we were grateful for a home that was quiet, safe and an oasis away from the world. It was something we really needed after all we'd been through during the past two and a half years.

On the Sunday we went to church together. It was a strange experience seeing everyone again. I wondered why it seemed we'd been away for twenty years. I didn't understand why I kept crying all the time, and found the service very hard to cope with. While singing the choruses, I tried to ask God what all this meant. How did it affect the lives of the street children and those around the world who were dying and in need of love?

After the service I spoke to a lady who asked me how things had been in Guatemala. I tried my best to say that it had been a wonderful experience. But I felt like shouting out, 'Don't you understand there are people dying out there?' I asked what things had changed since we had been away. 'Not much,' she replied.

A friend of hers came over to talk to her. They chatted together as if I wasn't there. It was a great tragedy. Their major topic of conversation was the fact that Tesco's had changed their aisles around and how hard it was to find anything. I left in tears, wondering how I would ever fit back into this life.

British Christians feel they are rich. In actual fact, the wealth is just like props on a big stage. What we now need is the script so we can see the reason for the props. When we do, we might realise that the props aren't needed in this play at all, but belong to another play and one in which we don't have a part. When we put Jesus and his agenda centre-stage, then we see things in their proper perspective. Then we can continue with the production.

We know the plot and how it will end. But those watching, our audience, do not. If we acted it out according to the script, the audience would engage with us. They would see the point to the play before the final curtain falls.

We had been contacted by a man from the church we used to go to in Guatemala City. The man had a plot of land that he was looking to sell. He wanted to know if we were interested in buying it as the site for a children's home. Some initial communication began between us and the owner of the land, mainly through the ministry in Guatemala.

We decided to wait until I could see the land with trustee Gary Grant when we visited Guatemala within the following two months. In the meantime we prayed and sought God's will on the matter, asking him for the money that would be needed to buy the land and build the home.

Meanwhile we had begun to collect the few things we'd left behind in storage in the UK and settled into our new home. Every hour I would look at the clock and work out what time it was in Guatemala and what everyone would be doing there.

We also collected from Ian Edwards all the paperwork that had been gathered since The Toybox Charity had been set up. There were many letters to answer, people and churches to write to and thank for their support over the past three years. We'd had invitations from some churches and schools to speak about our experiences. So we needed some sort of publicity material rather than the small photocopied sheet which we'd used previously.

The Toybox trustees met and discussed with us the way forward – how we were going to live, how we were going to get around, the plans we had for the future of Toybox and El Castillo and how much it would all cost. God had clearly guided us back to the UK, had confirmed it through a prophecy and provided us with a home. He'd also spoken to our church, St Leonard's, about supporting us financially – together with Christchurch in Tunbridge Wells. Christchurch was where I'd first become a Christian, back in 1981.

Just before the trustees' meeting, a businessman and his wife asked me to go and collect a car for them from a nearby Ford dealer. They asked me to look over the car for them before signing for it – not that I knew a lot about cars! I thought it was great and brought it back to them. When I announced that I had returned with their car they told me that it was now mine and was to be used to promote the ministry. God had provided yet again!

Together with the trustees we planned the coming year: return trips to Guatemala, the training centre, possible purchase of land and construction of a home for street boys, establishing an office in our spare room, and our roles as representatives in the UK for Toybox. It was a great meeting as we dreamed together and brought those dreams to God. After the meeting we started to get some things together for the office in our spare room: a desk, filing cabinet, computer, and so on. It was the start of The Toybox Charity UK – something that had been around before, but which now had our full-time attention.

A few local radio stations and newspapers made contact with us. They'd heard that we had returned and wanted to write an article on us or interview us on their programme. That led to more interest and more visits to churches, schools and interest groups. That in itself brought in many letters each week which we tried to answer as quickly as possible.

I was travelling around the country speaking. Jen

remained at home to cope with phone calls and letters. As the months went by, it became clear that we weren't coping with the response to our growing profile. Each new presentation brought in about ten letters. Each presentation might lead to another presentation which would lead to more letters, and so on. We needed help! So we were grateful when Angela Haward offered to work in a voluntary capacity for us, three mornings a week.

In Guatemala, the staff were awaiting my return and keen to look at the plot of land that had become available. It was wonderful to be back in Guatemala. I was excited to see the training centre, the staff – and of course, the street children. I was driven to The Tower where we unloaded the many bags I had returned with – thanks to American Airlines. The next day we went to see the plot of land that had been offered to us. The following week Gary Grant joined me and we looked over the land together.

It was situated high up in the mountains, about twenty minutes outside Guatemala City near the main road to Antigua. It was perfect for a home, far enough out of the city, but not too far for transport, shops and school. We walked over the land and prayed over it, and we knew deep inside it felt right.

On returning to the UK, Gary and I talked and prayed with the trustees about the land and the construction of a home there. The plot was large enough for us to build another home at some stage in the future if we wanted. Just before we met, we had confirmation from a group of volunteers from the United States who just happened to be planning to go to Guatemala in the summer vacation and help with a construction project.

The trustees agreed to purchase the land and plan the building of the home. As we prayed, money started to come in. Within a few months we'd bought the land and had begun looking over possible plans for the scheme. Work began that summer when the group from Siloam Springs, USA, arrived ready to give a couple of weeks' hard graft.

I'd managed to return to Guatemala in the June, just before the team arrived, so I could help plan the beginning of the construction. Getting the planning permission seemed such a formality. We had already been given permission to build a store on the site, which was heavily overgrown with trees. The permission allowed us to cut down trees for the building of the store; someone from the council would arrive the next week to assess the needs for a formal application for the house itself.

The team arrived from the USA and wanted to begin straight away. On our first day up at the site someone from the council came and told Mauricio, who was now our project co-ordinator, that there would be no problems. Then, seeing the group of Americans, he said it would not be possible to build, but for a certain gift he could arrange it.

We weren't getting into bribes, but thought and discussed the best way forward. Was it right to pay money to him just to get the permission, or not? God showed us that we needed to trust him and have wisdom.

A few days later we were given permission to build – so long as we didn't cut any trees down! That was impossible. The trees grew so closely together, the house wouldn't be any bigger than a metre square. But we had permission to cut down trees for the building of the store. So we began with the store, but kept changing our mind as to where it was going to go. By the end of the week we had changed our minds so much that there was now lots of ground free of trees ready to build. So work began, even though it was only to build a store room for the materials.

The architect and engineer – who'd both donated their time to us free of charge – started work on the plans. But we got into problems with the design process. It proved to be a disaster. The house ended up being built nearer to the road than was originally planned, and that meant losing the store we had built. It took about a year to complete. The budget soon ran out and a revised one was drawn up, and then another revision and another.

It seemed the home would never be built, but we finally completed in June 1996. The following month a family moved into the home, and we began to offer places to street children who'd attended the training centre over a period of a month or more.

The boys moved in with screams of joy and excitement as they raced around the property before settling down for an evening meal. Those first few months were a real strain for the young family who had moved there. The children stole various things from their rooms, woke in the middle of the night and broke into the cash box. The boys fought and tried to stir up friction between the father and mother. It was a challenging time for all those in the home as boys came and went. Sometimes those who'd run away returned in the middle of the night and enticed the younger boys back on to the streets, or sold them drugs.

We knew we had to pray and seek God's protection over the home, as well as doing something about the situation. It was hard for us to understand why the children would react to love like that. Even though I could totally understand where they were coming from, I could not see how they could reject the only and probably last chance they had to change the course of their life.

On that very first day with the street team in Guatemala, I had learned to keep my sights low, expect little and then I wouldn't be disappointed. But I knew that God's power was sufficient to change the most impossible of situations. How was it, then, that these children who had tasted the goodness of God could now reject it and in their anger turn others to their point of view?

I didn't collapse amid the debris. But I spent many hours alone, wondering if all this was going to come to nothing after all. Perhaps those people were right – the ones who had warned me about the folly of thinking that I could make a difference. Why was this happening? It seemed like another attack from the evil one. And for a brief moment, it seemed one battle that he might win.

10

The Miracle Is Still Unfolding

Marleny decided to run away. She'd been with us for a few months, staying at our brand new girls' home. But she thought she couldn't cope any more. So one night she gathered a few of her things together and quietly opened her bedroom door, which led to the garden.

As she crept along the path she looked back at the home. She told us later that as she turned to take in that final view, she saw two angels hovering above the home. Immediately she ran back in! She knew God was with her.

The boys' home was now up and running. But it had its own colourful history – even before it was set up.

The staff had learned some valuable lessons during the first few months on their own. Yet they were convinced that regardless of how the children treated them, they would show love to them. However, that didn't mean they would allow the boys to walk all over them!

They would set guidelines. And if the boys strayed from those guidelines, they would be allowed to seek forgiveness or choose to leave the home. Slowly the home grew more stable and became a safe harbour to many who'd spent too long in the storms of life.

Back in the UK, interest in the charity was growing rapidly. Money was coming in for the construction of the home, as well as enough for the running of The Tower and street teams. I found that God could use even me to do something I was never any good at and had the most fear of – and that was public speaking.

Many children were challenged as I travelled around schools. I told them about what Jesus had done in my life; how he had shown me the children who lived on the streets; and how he'd enabled me and Jen to help them. Here are some of the youngsters' comments:

Thank you for speaking to our school. I like you. Love from Casper. P.S. I had a good time.

Thank you for coming to talk to us. It was really really good. Please help the street children and we will help you. Love, Sally.

I am writing to tell you that we have raised £100 for the street children of Guatemala and were wondering how we can help them more. We did a bring and buy sale and raised £50. Our headmaster gave us another £50. Hope this will help with your work. From Rebecca.

I really thought that the true story we heard on the radio was good because you're thinking about other people and not just yourself. I wish I could help other children. If I had to pick a hero, it would be you. Yours faithfully, J.B.

Can you come to school for assembly with us? And tell us about the club you are doing in Guatemala and show us pictures about it for school? I feel sorry about the children who have no homes and I would not like to be like them. So please help them. From Jenny.

Thank you for coming to our school. It was very interesting, and it would be nice if you could come again. From what I've heard, Guatemala is a very nice place and I would like to go there, but there you are. I think you have done a lot to help the street children and I admire you going all that way to help them. That makes you a very good person to me. Thank you, Antonia.

I remember speaking, at one school, to a group of ten-year-old boys. I'd told the lads some of the stories of how God had provided for us in miraculous ways. During the morning break I joined the teachers in the staff room for a cup of tea. When I returned to the classroom, three boys came up to me.

'It's all true what you said,' they admitted. 'During break we phoned up your vicar in Tunbridge Wells and asked him if it was true, and he said, "yes".'

It was incredible to think that they'd taken it so seriously they were prepared to check it out for themselves. I didn't realise it then, but God was opening up this new area of ministry for us in the UK. And it was one that we'd never even planned. But it was one we were definitely excited about.

During our time in Chesham Bois as youth and children's workers, we had spent much of our time in schools, talking to pupils about the reality of God. We never thought we would have the opportunity to do it again. But it was that area of ministry that helped us get through a difficult first year away from Guatemala.

Jen and Katelyn had settled back into life here more easily than I had. It took me almost a year before I could face shopping in Tesco's! I found it hard to look at all the things on offer on the shelves – and then to think of those children I had seen looking for an apple core among the rotting rubbish of Guatemala City dump.

Many more schools were inviting me to speak about my experiences. And I put those into a context of faith in Jesus, who is alive today and who wants a living, dynamic relationship with each one of us.

That Christmas marked our first whole year back in Britain. The year had been full of challenges, conflicts and joys. But at all times we knew God was in total control. At the back of my mind was the thought that at any moment God was going to call us to go to another country – like Colombia.

It was just before we'd returned that two of our staff were invited to Colombia to view a couple of different projects there. As people started to get to hear of our ministry, we received invitations to speak at conferences in Central America and were asked to help support other projects.

God began to show us there was much to do beyond Guatemala, and that we were to be a blessing for many nations – not just Guatemala. But that would come in time, when those who had experienced the power of God for themselves could in turn go to other nations and demonstrate the love of God there.

So amid all this greater potential for an international work, I didn't want to enjoy living back in the UK! I just knew I would start enjoying it again, and then would have to leave it all and go off somewhere else. The Grants, who had given us the use of their annexe, asked me why we hadn't decorated it and made it our own. It wasn't through lack of time. I just found it hard to acknowledge that God would give us good things – and that he wanted us to actually enjoy them

In mid-February Gary and I returned to Guatemala to

evaluate the ministry and make plans for the coming year. The boys' home continued to be a struggle. However, some boys were making encouraging progress. One boy, Luis, had even gone back to live with his family. But now we wanted to open a home for street girls. And we had the feeling that this was something God wanted us to trust him for during the year 1996.

Gary and I looked at various properties that had been suggested as suitable for the new girls' home. We really liked one particular house, and made an offer on it. We didn't have the money to buy it. We just knew that if God wanted the deal to go through, it would all work out. Well, it didn't!

Just as Gary returned to the UK, the owner of the house phoned us. He said he'd changed his mind and wanted more money for the house. So we were left to decide whether to go ahead with the purchase at a greater price.

Gary and I talked with the trustees when I returned to England. None of us had any peace about it. So we decided to let the property go and say no. The Guatemalan staff were frustrated because they'd been planning to invite girls to the home a few months later. But time confirmed this to be the right decision, even though at the time it was a painful one.

During that time the ministry came under intense spiritual attack – one of many we face all the time. Our minibus was shot at, putting it out of action for a while. One of our volunteers was attacked in the street. Another was stopped by a policeman and robbed!

The workers arranged a night of prayer at the centre. They also went out on to the streets to pray in the different areas where we worked with street children. At the height of the problems we were representing The Toybox Charity at New Wine, a Christian teaching event in England. News of the difficulties hit us hard. We couldn't carry on manning our stall while the team were going through tough times back in Guatemala.

We put up a sign over our stall to inform everyone that we would be closed that day. Then we encouraged people to join us for prayer and fasting in one of the offices on site. It was an incredible day. We prayed for hours about each area of the ministry. And we sought God's protection over each worker and each child.

Various people dropped in throughout the day to pray with us. Some had prophetic pictures and verses of scripture that reminded us God was in control. Three young children said they received a vision for us. They came to where we were praying to encourage us. Amid the darkness, the young children said, God's light was breaking through. His kingdom was coming, and would become a more powerful force in Guatemala than ever before.

The following day brought news from Guatemala. Into every situation we'd prayed for, God had responded. Now we could rejoice that things were very different from the previous day. For when we call out to God, he promises to do something about it.

Meanwhile, the day-to-day work with the children continued to increase – as did the number of girls who were pregnant or caring for babies. We continued to ask God for a home for the girls.

In the UK it was becoming impossible to continue working from home. Our spare room had grown out into the hallway, our bedroom – and one of the stables in the grounds! It was time for us to look at alternative accommodation for the charity – and the increased number of people willing to help with mailings and other administration.

With Angela Haward's help, we tried hard to keep up to date with the growing number of letters each week. But we'd reached the stage where we needed someone full-time in the office. We'd decided it wouldn't be right to use the charity's money to pay for UK expenditure. However, that was now proving difficult.

We also wanted to keep to our promise of never writing a 'form' letter – including the name of the person we were writing to and just changing the amount on the letter which would correspond to their donation. But how could we do that on our own, and with our present system?

The trustees agreed to advertise for a full-time administrator. At the same time we prayed about alternative office accommodation. The following week we began to receive phone calls from prospective employees, all of whom looked just right for the job.

Then the local toy shop company owned by Gary and Cath Grant asked us to consider taking over an office in Amersham. The place had recently been ruined by a serious water leak, and the company who were renting it had moved to another location. It was available within the month – free of charge, for five years!

We began to interview a whole host of people who thought they were the right ones for the job. But they couldn't all be the right ones! So we prayed and asked God to confirm his choice. We chose a lovely lady called Margaret Byatt. We felt she would offer something very special to the charity as we took this next step forward.

Margaret lived in Chesham. She and her husband were regular members of an Anglican church there. Her heart was for children and she felt God had led her to us. She started in April 1996, in the same week as we moved into our new offices. God provided much for us in the way of stationery, desks and other office furniture through a company based in Luton that wanted to donate furniture to a charity.

It was amazing to see people and companies responding by donating a photocopier, computer equipment, chairs, fire extinguishers and even plants. A couple of weeks after we moved in, we had no more material needs. Everything had been supplied, for which we thanked God.

As the months passed by rapidly, it was time to begin planning my second return trip of the year to Guatemala. We'd been asking God for land for the girls' home. So that was one of the main things I wanted to look at during this forthcoming trip. I'd be in Guatemala for two weeks and would be joined by Nick and Kate Austin, a young couple from Surrey who had business contacts with the Grants. They'd shown an interest in the charity's work and wanted to see first-hand what we were doing.

In one of our prayer letters I'd mentioned that our next project would be the girls' home. A short time before I left for Guatemala, I received two letters from supporters who said they'd been praying for the girls' home. They felt God had said something to them which they needed to pass on to me. I read their letters – which described their vision of the land – then placed them in the back of my Bible.

'When I visit this time,' I wrote to Mauricio, 'I want to look at some different plots of land on which we could build a home for street girls.'

I knew what the boys' home land had cost us, and so was expecting to pay about £25,000 for a decent-sized plot. On arrival in Guatemala City I was keen to ask Mauricio about when we were going to start looking. He informed me there was only one piece of land to see – and that I could see it in the morning. I had come a long way and wanted to look at different options, not just one plot of land. So I expressed my concern.

'But this is the plot God wants for us, Duncan,' he replied.

He went on to tell me, as he, Nick, Kate and I drove up to the land the following morning, that he had been invited to speak on a Christian radio station. After the interview, a listener called him to ask if he would like to purchase a plot of land from him. He felt God was leading him to sell it to us. Mauricio and Herbert had been to see it and really felt that God's hand was on it.

We left the main routes after a forty-five-minute drive south from Guatemala City. The road became even more bumpy, especially when we passed the little village school and communal washing facility.

Guatemalan countryside is green in the rainy season – and fairly dry and brown the rest of the time. The further south you travel, the greener everything gets. There are hills that have been cleared of trees for farming. Small plots divide the land, which produces a variety of vege-tables, fruit and the very popular coffee plant. Even though the slopes of the hills are very steep, land is cultivated in steps.

The occasional goat or cow is chained up by the side of the road, or at the edge of someone's property. Adults and children work the land, bending over for hours on end pruning or planting, ploughing by hand or with a small plough pulled by a horse or donkey. Young children carry huge loads of wood on their backs or heads, rarely stopping for a rest as they struggle home or sell the wood by the roadside.

We headed up an unmade road, bouncing from side to side, trying to look over the high banks on either side. When we drove on to the land I felt my spirit jump inside. We climbed out of the minibus and went to view the plot.

Mauricio was eager to show us around. It was idyllically situated on top of a range of hills, with a beautiful view of the countryside below which was divided by the Interamerican Highway. The land started flat, dipped about a metre and then levelled off again. A small brick-built house was to the left of where we were parked. Below that were four small tin shacks, home to a young indigenous family who were acting as guards and caretakers of the land in the owner's absence.

It was beautiful. As I looked over the land in stunned silence, I remembered the letters from two families in the UK about this plot of land. Both had received what I can only describe as a vision of this very site and had described the location, the view, the contour of the land – even down to the number of trees on it! It was incredible to see something that two families had seen only in a prophetic picture.

Nick and Kate were very impressed. They asked me where we were going to get the money from to buy it. I tried to explain that we were going to pray! Mauricio came back to me after talking with the family who were currently living on the site. He asked me if I liked it and explained that the owner wanted the equivalent of £25,000. Those two weeks passed quickly as we began to make plans.

When I returned home I was desperate to tell the trustees all about the land. To the agenda I added: 'Purchase of Girls' Home £25,000', along with the usual things like finances and reports. The day after I returned, the trustees met at our home and we sat down for a meal together, waiting for the arrival of Ian Edwards. The doorbell went. Ian came in, apologising for being late. He looked down at the agenda on the table as he banged down a load of files.

'I have to tell you,' he said, 'that Toybox is broke! We

have no money. We need to seriously consider what to do next. And you can forget this!' He pointed at the item on the agenda where it mentioned the purchase of the girls' home for £25,000.

So the meeting didn't exactly start with a bang – except for Ian's files hitting the table! Yet I had learned that in the end God's will is done. So I sat back while the trustees discussed finances. And deep down I knew that what was impossible with man is possible with God. Eventually, in frustration, I spoke up. I said that this was something God had very clearly led us to.

It was hard to know what to say next apart from, 'Well, let's pray'. So we prayed. And we continued to work our way through the agenda. Then came the time for me to talk about the girls' home. I explained how I felt God had led us to buy that particular piece of land. The trustees, Jen and I prayed together.

Then they agreed this was clearly something God was leading us to do. If God provided the money – which I was certain he would – we would go ahead and purchase it. That was a decision taken when Toybox had almost nothing left in the bank.

The trustees are a cautious group. That's essential for us as a charity in the cut-and-thrust of today's world. Yet when they feel God is leading us in something, they're happy to leave it in his hands and not worry about the money. God has put people on the trustee board who give it a wonderful balance. They keep my feet on the ground and prevent me from rushing so far that the day-to-day ministry may get overlooked.

After the trustees left that night, I picked up the phone and called Guatemala. To my joy, Mauricio answered. I told him all about the meeting and that the trustees had agreed to buy the land.

'I know,' he replied.

'What do you mean, you know?' I queried.

'Well,' he continued, 'the owner of the land came in today and wanted to know if we were going to buy it. So because we knew this was what God wanted, I said yes. So the owner then said he needed the money in three weeks' time. And I agreed.'

'You did what?' I asked. Things were certainly moving very fast. I awoke early the next morning to pray about the whole thing.

When I went into our new office that day, I thought of what I was going to tell Margaret. I explained how, at the trustees' meeting, we were told that Toybox had hardly any money in the bank, but that the trustees were going to buy a £25,000 property and we needed the money to be in Guatemala within three weeks. Margaret looked at me in disbelief, as she was just getting used to me at that stage.

'So,' I told her, 'you need to keep going to the post office box because we are going to pray this money in.'

'Yes, Duncan,' she said, and continued with her morning routine. She told me later how she went home that night and told her husband, Peter, that she would probably not work with us much longer since we didn't have any money left!

It is normal in situations like that for charities to run appeals. But we were so busy that this thought did not enter our minds, nor did we want it to. We prayed and trusted God to provide. We never had the time to send out a newsletter or urgent prayer request – nor did we have the opportunity to share our need in church.

Nick and Kate, who'd been touched by their recent visit to Guatemala, were organising a few fund-raising events. The rest of us were praying each day. And we all became overjoyed by the way money just started rolling in. People were writing from all over the country, saying that God had placed Toybox on their hearts – they knew we needed money at that time. Margaret was kept busy going to the bank over the next two weeks, banking no less than £25,000. God provided all the money in amazing ways, not just for the purchase of the land but also for the ongoing running costs. We knew again that what God says in his Word about trusting in him is perfectly true.

That summer, plans were drawn up for the development of the site. An artist in Guatemala drew a wonderful picture of what the land would look like when the home was complete.

It would be in four stages: the first stage would be to remodel the existing home and build three small double units on one side of the property; the second stage would be to build two staff homes and three more double units; the third stage to build a large dining room; the final stage to build one more staff house and three more double units.

Each of the double units would have two bedrooms and a toilet and shower room between them. Two girls could live in each room or one girl and her baby or babies. Because of the size of the site, we would have room to grow corn and vegetables, and keep a small number of chickens. It was all meticulously planned. We were keen to get on with it.

A month later I was invited by youth leader Mike Pilavachi to talk about the project at Soul Survivor – a large Christian youth event held in Shepton Mallet each year. Mike had taken a keen interest in our ministry, and was keen to support us in some way. A plug from the main stage seemed a wonderful opportunity to tell of God's provision.

Mike asked me how we were going to raise the money for stage one of the scheme. I said we would pray. We'd seen that when God's people prayed and God heard and responded to those prayers, we would need less money – but achieve much more. But when God's people weren't praying, and so God was not responding, we would need more money but achieve much less. We then prayed together for God to provide the necessary £20,000 for stage one.

After Soul Survivor, Jen, Katelyn and I returned home for a few days before returning to Shepton Mallet for New Wine, a Bible week for 8,000 adults. The phone rang.

'We've heard about your plan to build a home for street girls,' said the caller. 'Would you like a donation of £15,000?'

'I think we can cope with that,' I casually replied. The money soon arrived, as did the remaining £5,000. After the rainy season finished in Guatemala, which was October, work began.

We knew it would take about five months to complete. But we had to do something about the girls who were already coming off the streets and had nowhere to live. Some of those girls had babies and young children, or were pregnant.

Herbert had decided to act. He transformed the training centre into a hostel, offering a home initially to eight girls, two with babies. It was exciting to hear of how they were adapting to living in a home. And I was keen to see this in action the following week during my visit to Guatemala.

One thing I'd always wanted to do for the girls – since this was the hardest group to respond to our love – was to invite them out for a meal. When we had the club I had always wished we had the opportunity to take them out one evening to an expensive restaurant where they could enjoy a little treat. Now this seemed like the perfect opportunity. So, with Herbert, I planned a great night out.

The girls were happy in the training centre. But it wasn't the best place for them. They'd left the streets, but the streets hadn't yet left them. Aspects of street life still reared their ugly head in the home each day.

The first evening I was there, Herbert arranged for us all to watch a video. It was a true story about a gang of young people in Mexico and how they lived on the streets. One of the gang became a Christian. The rest of the film was his testimony of how Jesus had changed his life.

After the movie, Herbert showed the girls the painting of how we thought their new home would look. It was an emotional moment. Then I asked the girls to join me on the Saturday night for a meal at a top restaurant in town. I explained that they would have to get dressed up – at which they squealed with joy – and that Herbert and I would collect them around 7.00 p.m.

We arrived early at the training centre to shrieks of excitement from the girls, who were rushing about everywhere getting ready. Most had borrowed skirts or dresses from various members of staff and looked exceedingly beautiful. Decked out in suits, Herbert and I stood at the entrance next to the sparklingly clean minibus. One by one we took each hand and helped the girls into the vehicle. They thought it was a scream!

On arrival at the restaurant – in one of the most expensive parts of town – the girls were helped out of the minibus and escorted inside. I opened the restaurant door for the girls. Then I saw two hesitate outside as they looked to the roadside where some children were begging. The thought that only months ago they were living in the same conditions came to my mind.

The girls walked in with heads held high. No one even turned their heads. Now they were young ladies – not street girls seeking enough food or money to last them the night through.

The restaurant the girls chose was a fairly upper-class pizza place. It was beautifully decorated with green plants and exotic flowers which were native to Guatemala. The building was full of the city's landed gentry. The luxurious cars parked outside betrayed the fact that their owners were in the rich five per cent of the population.

It was mostly families or young couples who were eating. There was a small area at the back of the restaurant for children to play. Classical music was playing quietly in the background, which makes the customer feel they're not really in Guatemala.

It was a great meal. But the girls kept putting small amounts of food in napkins and hiding them in the folds of their dresses. I decided not to mention it, and asked one of the other members of staff to drive them back to the centre.

Herbert and I went on ahead and were waiting at the centre when the girls arrived. As each one got out of the minibus, we handed her a bunch of red roses. Then two student workers from the UK organised a short show for the girls. Afterwards one of the girls stood up.

'I just want to say,' she explained, 'on behalf of all of us, thank you for . . .' and with that she burst into tears.

In March the following year, 1997, the girls' home was opened. It consisted of one large house, with three smaller double bedroom units. The red tin roofs made quite a noise when it rained and water would run down on to the grass below. The walls were of basic building breeze block and painted white.

There was no fence around the home yet and it was a little too inviting to outsiders. But it was clear where our property ended and our neighbours' began, because theirs was all arable farmland and ours was clearly a construction site. Cement was being mixed just outside the front door, trenches were being dug around the new units and plumbing was being connected to the bathrooms.

At the far end of the property a small amount of corn was being planted. That surrounded the new water well which had been dug by hand – all forty metres of it! It produced about ten litres a second, through the submersible pump and into the water storage tanks at the side of the house.

The girls moved in and began to make the home their own. Another dream had come true.

Meanwhile the street team had begun to work with a new group of youngsters, who we termed 'high-risk children'. These children were in great danger of becoming street children as they lived in very poor areas, spending most of their time playing or working on the streets. During one of my visits to Guatemala I was invited to join the street team as they went to work with a group of high-risk children near the international airport.

As we drove into their very poor neighbourhood, the children came rushing out to meet us – about thirty in all. We sang with them, told them stories and then asked if we could pray for them. One little six-year-old boy sat on my knee. I looked into his sad face and asked how I could pray for him. He thought for a moment.

'Just pray that my dad doesn't come home tonight and beat me and my mum up again,' he said. It was such a simple request – but one that made a profound impact on my life.

After we'd prayed for the children, the street team took out the soup from the minibus. One of the team asked the children what they'd eaten that day. The children said that they hadn't eaten anything and were waiting for us to come with soup. It was their only meal!

The following week the team visited the children and found them playing a game called 'street team'. The children were acting out what the street team did with them each week! They called themselves after the names of the street team; some organised a game, then another would bring out a first-aid kit and tend the others' wounds, another would pray for the group – while another would lead some worship. It was a powerful scene of how much of an impact we had made upon their lives.

In all the excitement of the girls' home in Guatemala, we hadn't spent much time praying about our own needs of a home in the UK. The couple we were staying with, Gary and Cath, were planning to move to Chorleywood – about ten miles the other side of Amersham. We weren't concerned because they had invited us to move with them.

However, over Easter three people came to us and said they felt this move was not what God wanted for us, but for us to trust God for a home in Amersham. It was a big level of trust, but we knew God could easily supply all our needs – even a house in Amersham.

The following week we met with Gary and Cath. They were obviously upset by the news that we weren't planning to move with them but to look for our own house. I thought that maybe they would feel snubbed. But after some sadness we prayed together and sought God's will for our house.

Gary brought the trustees together, and they recommended that our best option was to look to buy a home for about £100,000. We would pray for the £20,000 deposit needed and try to obtain an £80,00 mortgage. When we'd first returned from Guatemala, our churches in Tunbridge Wells and Chesham Bois had supported us financially. Now we were to start looking for a mortgage, the trustees thought it best to pay us a salary that would be enough to cover the loan and our household bills.

Even though we didn't feel at ease taking money from the charity for our salary, we did so on the understanding that we would seek ways of raising the money for our salary through personal supporters. This was so we could give the money all to Guatemala, and not use any of it for UK expenses. So we set up Toybox Crafts, a trading arm of the charity, which would sell handicrafts in the UK and donate the profits of the sales to the charity to help cover the UK expenses.

Some people had written to us and said they felt God wanted us to buy a house with three bedrooms. We also wanted a house near to the office and the centre of town, a house with a garage, fireplace and a shower! That was our shopping list.

As we began to look around, it became clear that very little was available for £100,000, as homes are rather expensive around Amersham. We then started looking at homes up to £120,000. When we visited the estate agent we were asked how much we had for a deposit. We replied about £100. Her face was a picture!

She invited us to look at a three-bedroom house in Amersham which had just come on the market that morning. Apparently the owners had to been in a deal with someone else and had made an offer on another house, which had been accepted, but their buyer had pulled out two weeks before they had planned to move.

So we went to see the house, which was for sale at £118,500 and which we really liked. It had all the items on our shopping list. The only problem was that the owners needed to complete within two weeks, as their chain were expecting them to complete on Friday 6th June.

We spent the weekend praying about it, and felt we should put in an offer on the house on the Monday.

We met with various agencies regarding mortgages. It became clear that on our salary we couldn't raise anything like the figure we needed. The mortgage broker who was seeking a deal for us didn't know what to put on the form about the amount of the deposit. He didn't know where to put the words 'we are praying about it', and was quite taken aback by our comments that God was going to provide.

We continued to pray, and we were encouraged to apply to the Bucks Building Society for a loan of £85,000. With our offer of £117,000 now accepted by the owners of the house, we knew we would need a total of £32,000 for a deposit – £12,000 more than we had asked people to pray about. We also found that a further £2,000 would be needed for taxes, fees and searches.

So we continued to pray, asking God to confirm that this was his will, not ours. Over that weekend money began to come in from people who'd heard that we were praying about the finances. Once again we were amazed by the faithfulness of God's people.

We began that week by going for an interview at the building society. We told them clearly that our salary wasn't enough for a mortgage of £85,000, but we wanted one anyway. We also required a discount – and needed to complete the following Friday. They agreed!

So we were able to move forward. A friend put us in touch with a solicitor who is a Christian. I phoned him and said we needed his services to act for us in the purchase of a home, but needed it done cheap! The solicitor graciously agreed to reduce the fees by £150 and then prayed for us over the phone.

We began to pray more about the deposit. The estate

agent asked us to call in at their offices. They asked us how the mortgage deal was going. We said we knew it was all in God's hands – and to our surprise the lady agreed. Things were now moving forward and money was starting to come in for the deposit. By the end of the first week we had about £7,000 towards the deposit. But we didn't have time to update people to pray about the increase of the deposit, which was £32,000.

At the meeting with our solicitor, we told him we had about £7,000 for a deposit, and that God would provide the rest by the following week. He began all the legal paperwork and searches, and encouraged us with a prayer. As the second week began we received more money towards the deposit. Katelyn began to get excited as we shared with her every time a cheque came to us, and we thanked God together each day.

The solicitor wrote and said that a water search would need to be done. That would take up to three weeks, and he had written to the water company three days previously. When I phoned him he informed me that he'd received the survey from the water company in that morning's post, and thought it was a miracle! He even phoned the solicitor acting for the owners and said he knew that God was in all this.

At the end of the first week, we had enough money to pay the initial payment for the deal to go through. Then at the beginning of the second week we were praying for the outstanding balance of £25,000. I went into the solicitor's office on the Monday with a cheque towards that amount. He asked me how the money was coming in. I said we were still short of £25,000, but that it was only Monday and he didn't need the balance until the Thursday.

The day before the transfer had to be made to the solicitor, all the money came in for the deposit, leaving only £500 to be found for the remainder of fees, taxes and searches. Everything came in when needed. On Friday 6th June 1997, Jen, Katelyn and I were handed the keys to our new home.

Just a few months later I was on another trip to Guatemala, my third of the year. This would be one of the most exciting trips I had made.

The couple who were running the boys' home had decided that they could not continue because their own family life was deteriorating under all the extra demands that were being placed upon them. We prayed that God would provide a mature couple with older children to take over their responsibility. God heard our prayers and brought to the ministry a couple Jen and I had known previously, who were older and had been praying about this for a long time. Now their and our prayers were being answered.

The new couple, Victor and Dina, made an instant impact upon the home, transforming it into their home where the children were made to feel a welcome part of their lives. About this time the number of younger street boys increased and we also were asked to help with a few boys who were living at high risk of becoming street children.

Two of those children were Jose and Max. They had been brought to the home by their father who couldn't cope any longer with them, as he was a single parent. When they arrived, they looked totally exhausted and malnourished. Dina gave the boys a shower and clean clothes, followed by a hot meal. The next day their father returned to take them to a judge so that we could have temporary custody of them. When he saw his two boys, the father burst into tears.

"I can't believe you have such great love for children

who aren't yours,' he told the staff. 'I thought I was going to find them as I left them yesterday. But today I find them clean, fed and loved. I praise God for you.'

'Guess what, teacher?' the two boys told Herbert that morning. 'We had breakfast this morning. It was milk with some round things in [cereal!]. It was our first breakfast in weeks. Thank you.'

The home was becoming more stable and it was a joy to see the way God was beginning to use the boys. I was invited to stay at the home one night – which I did with pleasure. I sat and talked with the boys, played football with them and pushed them on their new makeshift swings in the garden.

That evening, after dinner, I was asked to sit and listen to them sing for me. The boys had written a song about how God had changed their lives and they wanted me to hear it and know how grateful they were to have a home which we call Emmanuel (God with us). This is a literal translation of their song:

I have come to Emmanuel with the purpose to learn and my life to change. Dreams that I dreamed about, goals to reach. They are coming to their final phase. If there is anything I still need to learn, that is Jesus is my final goal, this is more than just a passing thought. I will follow you, oh Lord, I will follow you with all my heart, until I say as your servant Paul, the race is finished and the victory I have won.

Their song made me cry. Those children – who we'd prayed over for many years – were now filled with the love of God. Afterwards the children gathered around me, laid hands on me and prayed for me. How could I ever do anything else with my life? These were our children. Miracle children. God's children.

I slept well that night until I woke in the middle of the night to hear screams coming from the next room where the smaller boys were. Since the screams only lasted a few seconds, I assumed it must have been one of the boys having a bad dream. So I went back to sleep.

In the morning I asked Victor why one of the boys screamed in the night. He told me that it was his fault. Each night he popped his head in to each of the rooms to check all the boys were there and asleep.

'As soon as I opened the bedroom door, little five-year-old Marcos sat upright and screamed,' he said. Victor spoke to him gently and he quickly went back to sleep. 'He does that often,' Victor added. 'When he lived on the streets he was raped.'

I couldn't believe what I was hearing. Who would want to do such a wicked thing to such a lovely little boy? Later that day Marcos told one of our volunteers from the UK that he had been a bad boy on the streets, doing bad things with men. It has taken us a long time to show Marcos that he was not to blame for what happened to him, that he was just an innocent victim of the full extent of man's sin. Marcos now sleeps through the night.

My most recent visit to Guatemala was to be another treat in the boys' home. I was invited to see their outreach evening. The boys and staff at the home had decided that they wanted to do something special to show their neighbours how God had changed their lives.

So they set to work producing flyers which were handed out in the streets outside the home and to each house in the neighbourhood. Posters were made by the children and plastered on every lamp post and tree within a mile of the home. Victor and Dina talked with the boys about how best to get people to come to an evening of drama, singing and testimony. The boys all agreed it was best to pray and trust God to touch people's hearts, and planning to expect between forty and sixty people.

An extra forty chairs were hired. The boys worked hard at building a stage in the living room/dining room area. Props were made, along with a set depicting the death and resurrection of Jesus.

The evening came and people began arriving at the home. When Victor went on stage to introduce the children he saw that they were not in their places. One of the staff went to look for them and found them in one of the bedrooms, kneeling down together praying. The boys were a little overwhelmed that over 160 people had turned up! There wasn't enough room for everyone to fit inside. Many had to look through the windows from outside to hear the good news of how God can change a person's life.

I returned to the UK with my heart full of joy. I was now seeing the beginnings of something very special. I knew that God wanted me to write about these dear children, so I began. Foremost in my mind were the children, especially those we had lost. This book is dedicated to them in the hope that it may inspire many to help their little friends left behind.

This book is testimony of our God. He has proved over and over again his faithfulness to us. What he says in his Word can be trusted, relied totally upon and lived out every day of our lives. The Toybox story has just begun. Our heavenly mandate is to continue in the same, demonstrating God's love to the lost, hurting and lonely children of Guatemala. We are called also to train our children in Guatemala to serve God and be prepared to trust him at all costs and for all things. These children are miracle children.

We know that God will use these dear children, as they are a testimony of his grace to a hurting and needy world. We know that he will accompany their testimony with signs and wonders so that the world may know there is a God able to save, there is a God willing to heal, there is a God ready to help in the most desperate of circumstances. And all of us, his miracle children, will join with all the company of heaven and proclaim for evermore that Jesus is King.

In the meantime, God calls us – as he called the Old Testament prophet Isaiah – to 'loose the chains of injustice and untie the cords of the yoke, to set the oppressed free and break every yoke'. Certainly through the work of Toybox we have seen the light 'break forth like the dawn' among the street children of Guatemala City.

If you would like to know more about the work of The Toybox Charity, or would like to book Duncan to speak to your school, church or group, please write or phone us at:

The Toybox Charity
P.O. Box 660
Amersham
Buckinghamshire
HP6 6EA

Tel: 01494 432591
E-mail: toybox@toybox.org
Website: www.toybox.org

Romanian Rescue

Sue Smith

Already with four sons of their own, Sue and Graham Smith feel passionately moved to adopt a Romanian child. They travel to Romania to find Robert Sanducan Toldea, tiny, gaunt and suffering from malnutrition. Unresponsive and unloved, he taps his head in the monotony of his cot-bound life.

They are at the outset of a bureaucratic nightmare in a culture they do not know. But they are also starting out on an incredible spiritual journey through the struggles and joys they are to experience. It is a story of immense faith and love, personal upheaval and deep friendships, and the developing life of a whole nation.

Sue Smith is a teacher and writer, living in York. She is on the leadership/pastoral team of her local church and also works with Rapport, the Foundation for Marriage and the Family.

0 340 69408 4

Thank You God

A Book of Children's Prayers

Compiled by Lisa Potts

Lisa Potts, the brave nursery nurse who suffered injury while protecting infants in her care from an attack by a man with a machete, has compiled this book of children's prayers. The prayers have been written by children from St Luke's School, her Brownie pack and her Sunday School on all aspects of life: happy days, sad days, families, holidays, pets, peace, forgiveness, caring for others.

In her introduction she talks about what has motivated her to compile this book, her experience at the school, her love of the children, and her faith. THANK YOU, GOD is a lovely book to read with children and the perfect gift.

0 340 70981 2